A Joyful Embrace

A Memoir

Written by Dixie Frantz

FIRST PAPERBACK EDITION FEBRUARY 2023.

Author website: www.dixiefrantz.com; Instagram: @dixiefrantzauthor

Cover art and book layout designed by Sasha Ichoonsigy.

Angel wings art quilt on the book cover is the original design of Dixie Frantz at lifesloosethreads.com. Longarm quilting was performed by Lisa Taylor.

Author photo by Studio Pod-Houston. Interior photographs are family photos except for Mimi's high school graduation photo by Scott Tate Photography.

ISBN 979-8-9873377-1-4 (hardcover)
ISBN 979-8-9873377-0-7 (paperback)
ISBN 979-8-9873377-2-1 (ebook)

Printed in the United States of America.

This book is dedicated to Melanie "Mimi" Anne Frantz...
one heck of a great little hugger.

Contents

Introduction

PART ONE

Chapter 1   Where Do I Begin?

Chapter 2   Between the Cheesy Layers

Chapter 3   So Much to Learn
The Tribune – *You Gotta Laugh* – *"Anyway You Say It... Dorable Is Still Adorable," published 4/11/2007*

Chapter 4   The Wheels on the Bus Go Round and Round
Chicken Soup for the Soul Celebrates Teachers – *"Mrs. Keeling's Class," published in 2003*

Chapter 5   Mimi Gets Physical
The Observer – *You Gotta Laugh* – *"Hospital Stay Tests Survival Skills," published 1/24/2001*

The Tribune – *You Gotta Laugh* – *"Ode to Heather," published 7/14/2014*

Chapter 6   The Spirit Moves Her
The Tribune – *You Gotta Laugh* – *"The Hug Doctor Is In," published 9/12/2007*

The Observer – *You Gotta Laugh* – *"Christmas Pageants and Angels," published 12/22/1999*

PART TWO

Chapter 7   Mimi's Close Peeps

Chapter 8   Awkward Middle School Years
The Tribune – *You Gotta Laugh* – *"It Is a Lot Like Eating Liver," published 7/31/2013*

Chapter 9   Child Protective Services Comes Knocking

Chapter 10   It's a Wonderful Life
The Observer – *You Gotta Laugh* – *"Scoring a Home Run in the Game of Life," published 6/7/2000*

The Tribune – *You Gotta Laugh* – *"Zip Lines and Boas," published 8/17/2011*

Chapter 11   The Stars Align in High School

The Observer – *You Gotta Laugh* – *"Mums, Dance Dates Herald Fall Homecomings," published 9/18/2002*

The Observer – *You Gotta Laugh* – *"Teachers Make Prom Happen for Special Seniors," published 4/26/2006*

The Observer – *You Gotta Laugh* – *"Riding the Roller Coaster Toward Graduation," published 5/31/2006*

Chapter 12   Life at the Village

Chapter 13   Making Mimi's World Flat

PART THREE

Chapter 14   Living by the Rules

Chapter 15   The Simple Life

The Tribune – *You Gotta Laugh* – *"A Beautiful Day in My Neighborhood," published 2/25/2015*

The Tribune – *You Gotta Laugh* – *"Ho-Ho Is His Name," published 12/5/2016*

Chapter 16   A Scary Diagnosis

Chapter 17   Our Lives Sadly Change Forever

The Tribune – *You Gotta Laugh* – *"Mimi's Legacy," published 10/30/2018*

Chapter 18   Difficult Days Ahead

The Tribune – *You Gotta Laugh* – *"The M&M's That Bind Us," published 11/27/2018*

Chapter 19   Life Without Mimi

Chapter 20   Life is Not for Sissies

Final Reflections

Epilogue

Acknowledgements

References

Introduction

I started writing this book three months after our Mimi earned her fluffy angel wings. She unexpectedly left us on Wednesday, October 17, 2018. She was just thirty-four years, three months, and four days old. Perhaps this is my way of working through the intense grief that has left a huge hole in my broken heart.

This is a book from a loving mother's perspective about a daughter born with cerebral palsy and how she affected our family and the outside world swirling around her. Our Mimi also left behind a loving father, adoring older sister, and younger brother, as well as lots of extended family, friends, parish family, former teachers, therapists, and so many others.

The core of my story includes our immediate family of five. Mimi was our middle child. Rick was her father. Katie was Mimi's big sister by four years. Her little brother, Ricky, is three years younger than Mimi. We mostly lived in the suburbs just northeast of Houston, Texas. There was a brief year lived in Michigan, where Ricky was born. We have attended the same Catholic church in Texas since before Mimi was born.

My story is not unlike the stories of others whose mothers, fathers, sisters and brothers, guardians, and caregivers grew up with a family member with special needs, either from birth or through an accident. I have had the privilege over the years to meet, and befriend, many who are on similar journeys raising their children with disabilities. Whether our children have special needs or not, we love them deeply and wish them to be respected, valued, and to live their lives to their full potential.

This book ends a year or so after Mimi tragically left us. I still can't believe she is not physically with us. Mimi left us too soon. I believe her mission on earth wasn't close to being finished — which is another reason for this book.

To those who never met Mimi, you would have loved her. She had the purest spirit and most loving heart. Everyone who has ever laid eyes on Mimi will certainly remember her. Not because of her wheelchair, or the big blue eyes and dimples. No. Maybe you would have noticed the long, thick, dark hair that in the last few years was streaked with a little gray, especially at the temples. Those things might have been the reason you first noticed her, but she was so much more.

Throughout this book, you will also notice that Mimi connected deeply to the traditions and spirituality of her Catholic faith in interesting and unconventional ways. She had this tendency to lock eyes with a person and draw them to her. It was quite something to witness.

Intellectually, Mimi remained about two years old. It was an interesting, challenging, and delightful combination that left many wondering — just who was this little girl? She challenged me every day of my life. I spent much of it always trying to reach deep down into Mimi's sparkly soul and find out more about who she was, what she wanted, and to learn from her.

This book is also about what it was like for a family to have a special needs child born into it. You will read about the lack of understanding governmental organizations often have for those with special needs. There are those who are supposed to assist the disabled, and lots of them do, but there are also so many roadblocks put up in our way. You will learn about the gigantic alligator-infested hoops we have to jump through to get a morsel of assistance. But there are many heroes and advocates in this wild and crazy world. I will also talk about them.

This is your chance to peek into the window of one family's life growing up with a child who just happens to have special needs. It is the "insider stuff" about families who live with such a daughter or sister, brother or son, and the challenges they face. It will also be a joyful, spiritual, and uplifting journey.

Hopefully, I will inspire you to look at this special population a little differently. It is my belief our daughter molded, shaped, and inspired those around her to live life to the fullest, joyfully, and with great love. A year after Mimi left us, people still tell me they pray to Mimi every day. Many times, friends have pulled out her "hug" card (more on that later) from their purse, or wallet, or church missal. It is very humbling.

If you are reading this book and just beginning your journey with a special needs child, take heart. It is not always easy, but what journey is?

PART ONE

Chapter One

Where Do I Begin?

Experience: that most brutal of teachers.
But you learn, my God, do you learn.

— C. S. Lewis

I was sixteen years old in 1969, and in the middle of my junior year in high school. Without a doubt, my favorite class that spring semester was mythology. The course work was fascinating. I mean — who doesn't love a bunch of great ancient stories? The teacher was engaging and excited about the subject.

I was also taking practical business courses like shorthand and book-keeping. Obviously, mythology nourished the right side of my brain.

Toward the end of the semester, I recall struggling with what to do for the final project. My class average was already an A, but the project would be 25 percent of our final grade. After lots of agonizing, I finally decided to combine origami with Greek and Roman mythology. Basically, I would summarize eight or nine myths and pair each with an origami folding.

Some of the pairings were easy. For example, the story of "Pandora's Box," where Zeus, the ruler of the gods, presented Pandora with a box (actually, it was a jar) that she was not supposed to open under any circumstances. Ultimately, we all know what happened. Pandora released sickness, death, and many other unspecified evils into the world. I paired the famous myth with an origami box. Easy. For "The Twelve Labors of Hercules," I used an origami folding of a bull for the part in the story where Hercules captures a Cretan bull. Again, easy. I remember wishing there were an origami option for the myth about Medusa — I loved that story — about the scary lady with lively snakes instead of hair. That would have been a showstopper addition to my project.

It wasn't long before I was running out of origami to go with the myths. For instance, the myth "Daedalus and Icarus" is about a boy who flew too close to the sun with his man-made wings held together with wax. He fell into the sea and drowned. I used an origami crane. I know — it was a bit of a stretch.

Several days before the end of the semester, my mythology teacher asked me to stay after class for a few minutes. Lots of compliments followed about how much she loved my project and especially the origami connection. But what the teacher said next caught me completely off guard.

She explained that she took the liberty of showing a special education teacher my project. She hoped I didn't mind. Apparently, they were friends. The special ed teacher wondered if I might part with the project. Her students could use the origami as a teaching tool for helping with their fine motor skills. They also would enjoy the stories. Of course, I said yes. But it got me thinking.

It was common knowledge there were special education students in our high school. I passed the heavy wooden door with the "Special Education" plaque each day on my way to class. But no one ever saw what was behind that door. All the other classroom doors in the school had small windows. So did the door for special ed. Only that window was entirely covered over in brown paper, so no one could peek in. Not a sliver of sunlight shone through that window. I checked the next time I walked to class.

I never saw anyone coming or going from that classroom. I reasoned the students must have come to class when the rest of the student population was already seated in their classroom. Clearly, they also left their classroom before the school bell rang in the afternoon. And I never saw anyone remotely appearing to have special needs in the cafeteria at lunchtime. I suppose they were eating lunch in their classroom. It was as if they were invisible — because they were.

Little did I know that fifteen years later I would have my first up close and personal encounter with a new member of the special needs population when our daughter, Mimi, was born with cerebral palsy.

—

Mimi was born on July 13, 1984, in Houston, Texas, at Texas Women's Hospital. She was full-term, weighing in at a very reasonable 7 pounds, 11.5 ounces. In fact, Mimi weighed 1.5 ounces more than her older sister had at birth just four years earlier. Her official name is Melanie Anne Frantz. The name Melanie means "dark-haired one." It fit her perfectly. She was our only child born with a head of thick black hair. Add to that those piercing big blue eyes from my husband's side of the family, and she was already such a cutie pie.

Did I mention her birth was basically unremarkable? At least from our perspective we thought it was. There were a few disturbing moments. When my labor began, my doctor was called away due to a family emergency. We were told Mimi was to be delivered by one of his colleagues. Before that day, I had never met him, which made me a little uneasy. My doctor had delivered Katie four years earlier almost to the day in the same hospital.

Partway through my labor, the labor nurse indicated there was a chance our baby might have a heart murmur. She pointed this out based on the heart monitor readout. There was a little discussion about this possibility, but not for long. Whatever was causing concern just seemed to evaporate. A heart murmur was never mentioned again.

After four hours of unremarkable labor, our sweet daughter was born. But Mimi didn't cry right away after birth like our first child. Mimi was whisked away down the hospital hallway. We were not told why, but no one seemed alarmed. This was so different than our experience with Katie. Rick and I bonded with Katie right after her birth for at least an hour. Warning flags went up in our minds but were quickly lowered when we were told everything was "just fine" with our new daughter.

The nurses would eventually bring Mimi to my hospital room, but it was many hours later. There was no mention of any health concerns. We asked. Her Apgar scores were recorded at 7 and 9, meaning she was in good-to-excellent condition. Apgar stands for "appearance, pulse, grimace, activity, and respiration." Basically, the Apgar test evaluates a newborn baby's health at birth. The quick test is performed on a baby at one and five minutes after birth. The one-minute test determines how well the baby tolerated the birthing process. The five-minute score tells how well the baby is doing outside the mother's womb. Nothing in her Apgar score led us to believe there was anything wrong with our newborn daughter.

Oh, and did I forget to mention Mimi was born on Friday the thirteenth? I have never quite decided if I was superstitious about it or not. Well, maybe a little. After her birth, for years Rick and I paused for a moment and sighed when a Friday the thirteenth popped up on the calendar. In any event, my husband and I were led to believe we were taking home from the hospital a normal baby, whatever that means. Little did we know that a few months later our lives would change dramatically when we learned she was not as normal as we thought. She would eventually be diagnosed with cerebral palsy.

I will admit, a few years later we were still angry, not knowing the reasons why Mimi was born with cerebral palsy. It was unsettling to be sitting at church on Sunday amongst hundreds of families and being the only one with a child in a wheelchair. How did this happen? Some days it didn't matter. But some days it really would have been nice to know why. Did someone connected to the birth do something wrong?

We eventually engaged an attorney to put the matter to rest and retrieved Mimi's hospital records from the day she was born. The attorney had a doctor who reviewed such files. It was determined that the doctor and the hospital staff most likely had nothing to do with Mimi being born with cerebral palsy. Of course, the doctor hired by the attorney also mentioned there was probably no reason for Mimi's Apgar scores of 7 and 9 either. Clearly, there was a reason Mimi was whisked away so quickly. On the other hand, if something improper had happened, it obviously was not noted in the hospital records. I imagine mistakes are covered up from time to time. We would never know. We eventually just let our anger go and focused on what we could control — helping Mimi live to her full potential physically, mentally, and emotionally.

—

Mimi and I were in the hospital for just twenty-four hours before we both went home. It wasn't long before I noticed Mimi was going to be a challenging baby, but I never suspected a disability. She cried a lot, and the nights were so difficult. She really resisted any kind of nighttime sleeping schedule, no matter how much I nudged her in that direction. There was no amount of rocking, patting, changing, or feeding that helped to soothe her or bring about nighttime sleep. I used up all the tricks in my "mommy toolbelt" that my mother had taught me. I soon became one tired new momma.

The baby reference book of choice back in the 1980s was good old Dr. Spock. My paperback version was well read, highlighted, and underlined. There were no mommy blogs back in the '80s. I figured the only thing to do was wait it out and power on. Each night held the possibility that both of us would get a few hours of sleep.

And then there were the ear infections. They appeared early on in her life, starting at the age of three months, one right after the other. It seemed I was always in that pediatrician's office for medication and follow-ups.

I couldn't say the exact moment I knew something was different about Mimi. But there were a few instances that caused me to wonder. It was right around two months of age that babies normally smile and will look their mommy in the eyes. Mimi did not. According to Dr. Spock, babies also coo. Mimi did not.

During one of my follow-up visits with the pediatrician, I remember asking if something was wrong with our daughter. The doctor indicated there could be "developmental delays," but not to worry. He mentioned that lots of times these things turn around in babies. This was the very first time in my life I had heard the phrase "developmental delays." I didn't have a clue what it meant. Remember, back in 1984, the internet had barely been invented. The doctor's answer was such an off-the-cuff remark. It was obvious to me he thought there was no cause for concern. The tiny hairs standing at attention on the back of my neck were a warning that told me otherwise.

A few weeks later, I remember sitting on the curb with my lovely neighbor, Becky. She lived across the street for several years. We were having a conversation about Mimi. Becky and I had much in common on the block. Her son Brandon and our Katie were the same age and best buds. As I held a fretful Mimi in my arms, the two of us watched the kids play in the cul-de-sac. It was an everyday occurrence.

I recall one day Becky and I were thumbing through Dr. Spock's book and commenting back and forth how something was just not right. We decided it would be a good idea for me to confront the doctor to understand what he really did think was wrong with our daughter.

The following week, Mimi and I were back in the pediatrician's office for yet another follow-up ear infection appointment. Just as he was about to exit the exam room, I steeled my nerves and stopped the doctor. I told him I was not leaving his office until he told me what was wrong with Mimi. It was time for him to fess up. He calmly turned around and told me it was obvious Mimi had been born with cerebral palsy. In fact, he had suspected it for some time. It was right before Christmas and Mimi was a smidge over five months old. He suggested bringing in my husband and chatting about moving forward.

Cerebral palsy was this huge mystery to me. I knew no one with a child with cerebral palsy. Heck, I did not even know anyone who had a child with a disability. This was information I did not know how to process. I couldn't just call my mom up for her wise advice on child rearing. I considered her an expert, and she was, but cerebral palsy was something different. This was nothing like when I got the measles in elementary school.

To make matters worse, I couldn't turn to the internet for speedy information. Can you imagine? I received all my information from the public library, which was sparse, and sometime later from United Cerebral Palsy in Houston via a mailed pamphlet.

I was so angry the doctor hadn't told me what he suspected was wrong. At home, Rick and I had heated conversations about the doctor withholding his suspicions. There were also lots of sleepless nights tossing and turning, thinking about what Mimi's future would hold. Mimi had sleeping issues and chronic ear infections, she couldn't hold up her head, and she was not rolling over or looking me in the eye. Lots of important milestones were already missed. And I didn't have a clue how to help our daughter.

I felt so alone without my mother to lean on. My mom turned out to be a huge cheerleader throughout Mimi's life. She had raised five children, and over the decades she helped me in so many ways. Unfortunately, she and my dad moved far away to the state of Washington. It was a job transfer that led to the move, which happened almost the minute Mimi was born.

—

It took three long months to get an appointment with a pediatric neurologist. I marked the days on the calendar with a big "X" until the big day that had so much power over little Mimi's life. Our major concern was that without an official diagnosis Mimi couldn't start treatment or therapy. Would he confirm what the pediatrician had suspected, or would we be led down another path? We didn't have a clue.

Rick and I, along with four-year-old Katie, drove into Houston with Mimi strapped into her car seat to meet with Dr. Zeller. Mimi's little head was cradled with small pillows on both sides as she had no head control. Most children by this age are crawling. Mimi couldn't even sit up.

After a short wait, the doctor examined Mimi. He confirmed cerebral palsy was Mimi's diagnosis. We learned cerebral palsy is a broad term for a condition caused by brain damage either before birth, during birth, or immediately after birth. The brain damage can be mild, moderate, or severe. It affects muscle tone, coordination, and control. Fine and gross motor skills can be affected. We had already experienced the classic signs of cerebral palsy — a delay in development and growth milestones.

Statistics show two to three children out of every thousand have cerebral palsy. We learned there is no cure for cerebral palsy, but it could be managed, and the life span of people affected by it was normal.

Dr. Zeller wrote a prescription for physical therapy and told us to start as soon as possible. He said there would be no need for further testing to determine what areas of Mimi's brain were damaged. In other words, she would not need a brain scan. The damage was what it was. He could not say how, when, or why the damage to her brain happened. There are lots

22

of reasons why these things happen, but they are difficult to pinpoint. I certainly didn't fit the profile of an expectant mother who drank excessive amounts of alcohol or did illicit drugs. Heck, I didn't even smoke!

The doctor told us that how far Mimi would progress in life with learning and physical abilities would depend a lot on her. It also would depend on us working with Mimi in tandem with the therapists. Dr. Zeller also admitted he couldn't peer into his sparkly crystal ball far out into the future and tell us Mimi would ever learn to talk, walk, read, or write. But she might. Cerebral palsy also did not mean Mimi would be mentally impaired, although sometimes that was indeed the case.

We went back to see Dr. Zeller for a couple of yearly follow-up appointments just to check in, so he could see how Mimi was doing. Mimi finally started to thrive health-wise. The ear infections became less and less frequent. But physically, not so much. Progress was super slow. We were eventually given the green light to drop our yearly visits with Dr. Zeller. He would always be available if there was a need for his services.

One of the lessons I learned from Dr. Zeller was that time is of the essence for children with disabilities. Starting therapy, which would be tedious and time-consuming, as early as possible could create some great outcomes. I would have much rather used those precious three months we waited for an appointment on Mimi's physical therapy. What a disappointment and waste of time Mimi's pediatrician created for us.

—

After our visit with Dr. Zeller, I don't know why I gave the pediatrician a second chance after I had to confront him about Mimi's cerebral palsy. Maybe it was because he was more than adequate when it came to the care of both our daughters. Perhaps I was overwhelmed in general and changing doctors just seemed too difficult. I do believe the pediatrician was doing everything possible for Mimi when it came to her persistent ear infections. But just maybe I am too nice. Yes, I know I am too nice. I rationalized that our pediatrician would now step up since we all knew cerebral palsy was going to be Mimi's huge challenge. In any event, I kept giving the pediatrician chances. But that was about to change.

Mimi was also having terrible issues with constipation. It didn't help that Mimi also had a horrible gag reflex and had a difficult time generally with most foods and textures. If I gave her anything that wasn't liquid or super smooth, it came right up. It was a challenge throughout her life to transition to what we liked to call "big people food." The gag reflex slowly resolved itself but eating off the kids' menu was pretty much standard fare for Mimi all her life. Thank goodness no eating establishment ever pushed back and made her eat off the adult menu. If they had, I probably would have cried.

The pediatrician's remedy for Mimi's constipation was always lots of apple or prune juice. Every time Mimi had an appointment for another ear infection, or another follow-up, I would also express my deep concerns about her chronic constipation. Each time he would look at me like I was nuts and push for more apple juice. He would eye roll in my direction more than once. I remembered being young and performing the eye roll on my mother, and she did not like it! Yes — the pediatrician's reaction was very offensive. But still I stayed.

Finally, during yet another ear infection follow-up visit, a doctor who was not our regular pediatrician entered the exam room. I don't recall if our pediatrician was on vacation or why exactly there was a different doctor in the room. It had always been a "one-man band" type of practice. Divine intervention? I like to think exactly that! I think God was so tired of me praying for a solution to Mimi's constipation issues. Again, I pleaded for some advice to relieve Mimi's constipation. He could tell I was upset by the tears welling up in my eyes. After a discussion about what remedies I had tried, he left the exam room lost in thought.

A few minutes later, he brought in a very thick book. It reminded me of a telephone book. I feel certain it had something to do with medications. Obviously, computer programs have today replaced this beefy book. But it was still the '80s. Not to mention there were no over-the-counter options such as MiraLAX. I watched as his index finger thumbed through multiple pages. Eventually, he reached for his prescription pad and started scribbling. It was a non-habit-forming syrup for constipation. I was to place the prescribed amount into her formula and shake.

It worked like magic. As crazy as it sounds, that first normal bowel movement after the prescription kicked in was the moment of my epiphany. Our pediatrician may have been great for "normal" children, but he absolutely sucked for Mimi. I never brought either of my children back to see him, and he never called to ask why. Okay, I really did not expect a call. The good news was that for a long time there was no more constipation. We stopped the prescription once Mimi started eating regular food. Constipation was not an issue until many years later when she was an adult. So much sitting in a wheelchair causes all kinds of bodily challenges.

I learned so much from the negative encounter with the pediatrician. Parents are the most important part of the team when you have a special needs child. Parents need to be like the conductor of an orchestra. We take our baton and let the symphony play in perfect harmony according to the sheet music. But sometimes you need to hit the offending violin player on the top of the head with your baton and show him the door. Actually, I would have rather thrown a tuba and a harp at him, but again, I am too nice. In a way, the stand-in pediatrician gave me a gift. If I was going to do a good job raising Mimi to reach her full potential, I was going to have to advocate for her. If a member of Mimi's team is not engaged, listening, or problem-solving, or if one of them happens to eye roll in my direction, they are shown the door!

—

Mimi started physical therapy shortly after our visit with Dr. Zeller and his diagnosis. She was just a tad over eight months old. Because both Rick and I worked full time, we started physical therapy at home. Ms. Joyce, a jolly older lady, came to our home in the evenings for an hour per session. She was short, with short gray hair.

I do not recall if it was once or twice a week, but I do remember lots of crying by everyone during therapy. Because Mimi didn't like the way Ms. Joyce was tugging and pulling on her, she screamed the entire therapy session. And Katie and I cried pretty much the entire hour also. Poor Katie was just four years old and probably thought Ms. Joyce was trying to kill her sister. It didn't matter how many ways I would explain to Katie that Ms. Joyce was not hurting her little sister — she still cried. I feel certain Rick was tearing up also, but I could never peer into his eyes while therapy was in progress, with all of us sitting on the family room carpet. Ms. Joyce was trying to teach Mimi to hold her wobbly head up, improve her trunk control, and roll over with various exercises and maneuvers that were new to us. As Ms. Joyce pulled and prodded, she taught us to perform these exercises and movements.

That first session was the moment physical therapy began to rule my life where Mimi was concerned. Obviously, it had to. It made me feel so sad. Mimi's childhood would obviously not be carefree and spontaneous but carefully orchestrated. I never played with Mimi from that day forward without thinking about the therapy component. I would ask myself if the activity I was about to perform with Mimi was going to improve her physically, mentally, or help with her fine motor control.

After the first visit, Ms. Joyce talked to Rick about building a little padded corner that would fit Mimi and stimulate her sitting up. It was for Mimi to practice sitting upright and improve her head and trunk control. Rick and I collaborated. By the next therapy session, a custom padded corner for Mimi was presented, according to Ms. Joyce's specifications. Rick built it in his garage workshop out of plywood. I was a beginner quilter and purchased thick, fluffy batting, the inner core of a quilt, to soften the surface of the wood. Then Rick and I covered the batting with a flowery light blue pre-quilted fabric. It wasn't exactly a masterpiece, but it was certainly our first of many collaborations on Mimi projects.

Did I mention the very first visit with Ms. Joyce was an assessment of Mimi from a physical perspective? It soon became obvious Mimi had a lot to catch up on physically. We knew that. But Ms. Joyce also mentioned something I will never forget. You see, Ms. Joyce had been working in the special needs trenches for decades. It quickly became obvious she had seen all kinds of children from all social and economic backgrounds. She did not mention specific stories. Those were confidential. I could tell by the look in her eyes the importance of her very next sentence. Ms. Joyce locked her eyes with mine, grabbed my hand tightly, and said, "Mimi is going to be fine." She told me Mimi would be loved by teachers and staff. I thought that was such an odd thing for her to say. I mean, how would she know? Our journey with cerebral palsy had barely begun, and Ms. Joyce seemed to be throwing me important words of wisdom? Then, she told me Mimi was "pretty, clean, and well-dressed." Perhaps Ms. Joyce was presenting me with a challenge. Mimi would get more attention because of how she was dressed — and smelled. It was a shocking statement that I did not take lightly.

—

In 1986, our little family of four moved far north: 1,175 miles to Kalamazoo, Michigan. The engineering job market in the Houston area had experienced a huge downturn. Mimi was two and Katie was six years old. I was not happy about the move. We still owned our house in Texas, and after not being able to sell it, we had no choice but to rent it out. The housing market sucked in 1986. That meant we would also be renting in Michigan. It wasn't long before Rick informed me the rental market was tough in Michigan. In fact, there was quite a shortage.

Rick flew up to Michigan for a few days and came home declaring he had rented a duplex apartment. He told me it was the only thing he could find. This took me back to our poor college days. Geez ... and I thought we had left that world behind years ago for single-family housing.

Several weeks before we were to make the move, my mom flew down from Washington to stay with the girls. Rick and I flew up to Michigan so he could show me around. One of our stops was of course the duplex. I gasped as he gave me the tour.

"Surely there is something better than this?" I questioned.

The one-car garage wasn't the worst part about the place. At least there was a spot for one of our two vehicles during the winter. Kalamazoo was known for receiving plenty of lake-effect snowstorms. It wasn't even the fact that our family was going from a house to a much smaller accommodation. I could live with that — kind of. There was a laundry list of non-negotiables with the place. The part that stuck in my craw was the total rustiness of the interior of the dishwasher. Sadly, it reminded me of my first car in high school. My dad made me buy it. The 1962 Chevy's original paint color was white. When I purchased the car in 1971, it was more rust-colored than white, and the radiator leaked.

Back at the hotel, I grabbed a local newspaper and circled potential rentals at lunch while Rick inhaled his burger. Afterward, I made Rick drive around to see if indeed there were any better living arrangements in town.

After a few hours, I threw up my hands. I should have trusted Rick. There really wasn't anything remotely better.

We wound up living for a year in what I called the "dumpy duplex." Our bedroom furniture, which wasn't chunky by any standards, only fit in the damp, dark basement near the washing machine and dryer. The girls' tiny bedrooms were upstairs. In the days before baby monitors, this caused me lots of anxiety.

And I did not fit in. I joined a Newcomer's Club. When I opened my mouth and my Texas drawl came spilling out, it was all over. I eventually dropped out after a fistful of meetings. Heck, I didn't really want to be in Michigan, and I suddenly became painfully shy. Not a great combination.

—

But Michigan was not a total bust. The good news was every state had early intervention programs designed for children with special needs. Typically, early intervention programs serve children from the ages of zero to three years old. Since I was no longer working, Mimi would be able to participate during the day. The goal of early intervention is simple. Children who are behind in skills receive the special services needed for them to start kindergarten, hopefully at the same level as their peers. I understand some state programs are better than others. It just so happened that Michigan had great programs, and Kalamazoo was exceptional in my book.

Mimi received services from two places each week during the school year. The first was in a cute little wood-framed house elevated with cinder blocks. An older lady had lots of toys scattered around on the floor. The best way to describe what went on there was play therapy. I would bet it probably has another name in the world of special education. The three of us — the lady, Mimi, and I — got down on the floor and played with toys. Or rather, we tried to encourage Mimi to manipulate a toy, any toy, by using her hands and fingers.

After the initial assessment, the lady also discovered Mimi was tactile defensive when rubbing on her hands and feet. It is difficult to explain tactile defensiveness if you haven't experienced it, but I will try. How does the sound of scratching your fingernails on a chalkboard make you feel? To many, that sound is very offensive. Is your skin crawling? Imagine that scratching sound on steroids, only it is related to touch. Now think about how hard it is to work with your hands, or walk, if you are very tactile defensive. Exactly.

Mimi was also very tactile defensive in her mouth. Certain food textures were just not tolerated at all. The dry and gritty texture of strained meat in baby food was one of them. It did not matter what smooth food I mixed it with, Mimi felt it in her mouth. Because of her extreme tactile issues, she didn't give up her baby bottle and baby food until she was four or five years old. Early on, those challenges meant feeding issues, and later, dental appointment challenges. Couple that with a bad gag reflex — you get my drift.

One of the gifts from the play lady was a small, simple quilt with lots of colorful square patches and a baby-blue backing. It measured twenty-five inches by twenty-two inches, and the layers of top, batting, and backing were tied together with white yarn. Each fabric square had a different texture: bumpy, scratchy, smooth, silky, fluffy, etc. The fabrics were leather, tweed, cotton, corduroy, and something that strangely reminded me of a Brillo pad. The play lady told me she made the quilts for all her little students. Apparently, tactile defensiveness was common. Having Mimi touch all these textures over and over was meant to desensitize the tactile nightmares in her little hands and feet. All these years later, I still have the precious little quilt.

Mimi also attended an early intervention program at Parkwood-Up-john Elementary in Kalamazoo. From the moment Mimi and I entered the school, I saw something unique and special. It was an elementary school that appeared to have just as many students with special needs as it did regular education students. Mimi's teacher told me special needs students were bused in from all over Kalamazoo to the school. I recall leaving with Mimi after a therapy session and seeing kids all over the playground. Lots of students in wheelchairs and using crutches or walkers, all playing together with ambulatory students. It was as if those walking aids did not exist. It made quite an impression on me.

Mimi received special services from that school's campus in the form of physical therapy and a circle-time type of activity. There was a teacher who facilitated a small group of parents with their children with different special needs. A couple times a week, we sat on the floor in a circle in front of the teacher. Our children sat in our laps, and together we sang songs while moving our children's hands. Songs like "The Wheels on the Bus" come to mind. We also played little games and tried to get our children to interact with each other.

Mimi and I also met separately with the teacher. In this setting we concentrated on getting Mimi to focus and use her hands and eyes at the same time and getting her to use simple sign language to "voice" her wants. I was also learning what things to reinforce with her at home. I learned to help with therapy that was meant to get her to improve not just physically but also with speech and fine motor control. It wasn't long until Mimi's six-year-old sister and her dad were also helping me at home with these activities.

Mimi also had physical therapy at the school on the days we came for circle time. The therapist had such a different way of working with Mimi compared to our first therapist, Ms. Joyce. From the first day, the therapist distracted Mimi with play while she worked. She might have a toy in one hand while getting Mimi to work on a physical activity that might cause her distress. The therapist had lots of equipment and changed up the activities all the time. It worked perfectly. Mimi no longer cried. I no longer cried. Mimi's responses were much more purposeful. Mimi made progress, but it was still so slow.

—

Despite my not fitting in, there were lots of fun times while we lived in Michigan. I remember teaching Katie how to make a snowman. As a child I had lived near Detroit and had some serious skills in that department. I made the girls matching dresses for Christmas from navy dot fabric with big white lace bibs. I also made the girls' costumes for Halloween. They both were Minnie Mouse. The duplex was one of about forty that were separated on large lots in a huge traffic circle. I remember loading Mimi into her stroller and taking the girls trick-or-treating in the neighborhood.

I was pregnant with Ricky almost from the moment we arrived in Kalamazoo. My pregnancy was never considered high risk just because Mimi had been born with cerebral palsy. I took Mimi to all my OB appointments, and when I learned we were having a boy, I tried to share the news at home. Rick dared me to keep the baby's gender a secret. For the next several months, I always told everyone Mimi and I were the only ones who knew if we were having a boy or a girl! Ricky, every bit of nine pounds, nine ounces, was born in Kalamazoo on May 6, 1987. Thankfully, my mom came from Washington to spend two weeks with us to help with the girls. I don't know what I would have done without her.

As I mentioned earlier, we lived in Kalamazoo only for one year. But before we moved back to Texas, the summer after Ricky's birth, Mimi's teacher and the circle time moms at Parkwood-Upjohn threw me a surprise baby shower for Ricky. We might have seen each other only briefly each week during the school year, but we were all floating in the same lifeboat with our darling children with challenges. Such a great group of ladies.

Chapter Two

Between the Cheesy Layers

I alone cannot change the world, but I can
cast a stone across the waters to create many ripples.

— Mother Teresa

I thought it best to stop here in my story to tell you a little something about myself — the person doing the writing and the mothering. And while Mother Teresa's quote does not in any way define who I am, it does inspire me to try to make a positive difference.

I believe that, like a great lasagna casserole, people are multi-dimensional, with lots of delicious layers. In that vein, after I wrote a humorous column for close to twenty-five years for several local newspapers, readers think they know me. They know parts of me, perhaps, like the stringy cheesy layers. They might not know how difficult it was some weeks to write 750 words on a deadline. Especially during those times when Mimi was recovering from another orthopedic surgery. Try writing something funny on those days. During the difficult moments, which everyone has, I really wanted there to be something to smile about. We either get through them with grace and humor, or those moments can rip us apart. I chose grace and humor.

For me, noticing the humor in everyday life surfaced when I married Rick. He is a very funny guy. It was the way he told a joke that first attracted me to him. The guy had a huge repertoire. He could tell me ten jokes in quick succession, and I knew he was just getting started. I was probably the perfect person for him. I never saw the punchline coming.

Rick's mannerisms and speech also endeared him to me. While we were dating, he had this funny thing he did when he applied the brakes on his car. He would take his hands and pull them back toward him as if making a horse slow down. Since I had recently moved from Colorado, it made quite an impression. His family was originally from Louisiana, and there were all kinds of words he pronounced in a way that tickled me. A library was a "liberry." A dresser drawer was a "draw." And a suitcase was a "grip." I know that last one is not about a different pronunciation, but you get my drift.

—

My interest in writing can probably be attributed to a teacher in the fifth grade. She made everyone keep a daily journal. The assignment was to last the whole school year. I think I was the only student not in physical pain at the mention of the assignment. To me, it sounded like fun.

Did I mention I didn't particularly care for this teacher? Her name was Mrs. Cowling. Funny how we remember details like that. She was an older lady with gray hair with a thick white streak through the center. Oh, and she had large nostrils, like a cow. I never saw her soft side. Maybe teachers needed to be tough with fifth graders. I don't know.

There was this twit of a boy who sat behind me who was so annoying. His desktop hinges were broken, and very often he used it to his advantage. When the teacher was facing the blackboard, the twit would quickly lift his desktop in my direction and hit me on the back of my head. Not so hard I would be knocked out, mind you. Of course, the teacher never saw him do it. I complained several times, but nothing ever happened.

Mrs. Cowling's journal assignment required her students to write one page in a notebook each day about anything on our minds. If I had thought about it, I would have written about the twit and the torture I endured at his hands. Perhaps she would have read it and intervened on my behalf. But probably not. I had decided to suffer in silence.

I enjoyed writing so much that I kept it up for many years after the fifth grade, in the form of more notebooks, and later, multiple diaries. There is a stack of old and dusty spiral notebooks in my closet that really need to be thrown away. A few times I have taken them down to thumb through the pages. They were loaded with incomplete sentences and misspellings and immature musings. And don't get me started on the handwriting.

As an adult, I gave up the daily journals but still wrote about special occasions and vacations in a fancy leather-bound journal. Photographs are fantastic but notes about what I was thinking and feeling added a dimension to the story. Life is in the interesting details you can't always remember through a photograph.

—

I did not attend college by the traditional route, straight out of high school. When I was about twenty years old, I worked as a receptionist and had various secretarial jobs while Rick attended The University of Texas at Austin. He already had a couple of years of community college hours under his belt when we moved from Houston to Austin. Those were some very lean and character-building years. After two and a half years in Austin, Rick earned his bachelor's in civil engineering. The year was 1976 when, on a wish and a prayer, with fifty dollars in our pockets, we headed back to Houston, towing a small U-Haul with our meager possessions.

Many years later, when our three children were in school all day, I decided to take classes at our local community college. I was forty years old. I loved college. Well, maybe not the government or the math classes — but the rest were life-changing! My favorites were the English-related ones, where I learned, much to my surprise, I could write. During my first English course, Composition and Rhetoric, the professor kept putting my papers on the overhead projector as an example of good writing. It was embarrassing, really. I just thought I had lots more life experiences than most eighteen- or nineteen-year-olds. I wrote it off as due to all the journaling over the years and to being well-read. My parents always had lots of great literature in our house when we were young.

I mostly took two classes a semester, studied at night while the hubby and the kids slept, and graduated in five years. My family all helped with my studies. Rick and Katie tutored me in math. Mimi was the subject of a final project in a photography class entitled "A Day in the Life of a Disabled Child." The photographs depicted little everyday events: Mimi getting a haircut and tipping the stylist, bowling with a ramp, walking around the block with her brother pushing her wheelchair, stacking blocks with her teacher, things like that. United Cerebral Palsy hung some of the original prints in their Houston office for several years.

Everyone in the class took black-and-white photographs with old-fashioned 35mm film and processed and printed everything in the dark room. Who knew the local community college had a great dark room? It was one of my favorite classes. I spent many happy hours in that dark room and hated to see the class end.

Even Ricky, still in elementary school, assisted with my college classes. He posed for photographs and even timed me around the track for a PE class.

It was also at the community college that I took a couple of mass communication and reporting classes taught by our local newspaper editor, the lovely Cynthia Calvert. We learned interviewing skills, *AP* (Associated Press) *Stylebook* guidelines for newspaper writing, laying out the newspaper before it went to press, and so much more. We were required to write several newspaper articles for the local newspaper. After my first story was published there, I learned what a rush it was to write and have my name appear as a byline. I feel certain not many people pay close attention to who writes a story, but I do. That class was a great way to be published and start a writing portfolio. I also had the opportunity to intern for the local school district, which involved writing many press releases and taking lots of photographs during the semester.

My favorite stories to write were features. One of my first was about a local chiropractor whose wife had died from cancer some years earlier. The wife was the inspiration behind his being a hospice volunteer. I sat in his office for the interview, and by the end we had both reached for the box of Kleenex on his desk numerous times. I was so humbled to be able to tell his story. I hoped I had done a good job.

Then there was my least favorite story. Everyone in the class was required to write a sports article. I was assigned a high school student who played softball. I remember sitting in her living room while her parents looked on. Saying the young lady was shy is an understatement. She barely said three words in thirty minutes. It was then I turned to the parents, who were forthcoming with some tidbits, so that I could fashion a story.

I started working part-time at the newspaper and was eventually offered a regular column. One day Cynthia asked me if I could write funny. I really didn't know. I told her I would write one and see what happened. I imagined it was going to be a little slice-of-life kind of personal essay on life in the suburbs. I certainly had enough family members to write about. But I thought that if things didn't work out, that was okay too.

Twenty-four years later, I was still writing. I loved that Cynthia never told me what to write or pulled a column she deemed not newspaper worthy. I had creative control over what I wrote and appreciated her support. They were not all masterpieces, believe you me! Maybe a handful were really good. When they were, Cynthia would email me and let me know. I have amassed well over 450 newspaper pieces over the years. The column, entitled "You Gotta Laugh," presented a mom's/wife's perspective on living in the suburbs. I know — the column title is lame. I had to come up with something on the spot.

About fifty of those "You Gotta Laugh" columns were about our little Mimi. I have included some of the columns in this book. It might be a tad on the serious side without them. As Mimi's mother, I had a unique platform to let readers peek into our family's window and used it when the opportunity presented itself. It was my little way to let people get a glimpse into the funny and special moments of what it was like to have Mimi in our family.

Over the years, I have had the opportunity to write press releases for the local school district, the community college, and a state representative. I wrote a blog post for MD Anderson Cancer Center, a "Chicken Soup for the Soul" story, and a feature for a national women's magazine.

In 2012, I also started blogging, mostly about quilting, some travel stories, and later Rick's cancer story — a cautionary tale.

—

Another one of my passions is quilting, which I discovered long ago, shortly after Katie was born. I recall taking a beginner class, before rotary cutters, special mats, and fancy rulers were invented. I learned the old-fashioned way with cardboard templates and scissors. My first quilt was nine squares and called a sampler. Each square was a different quilting pattern or technique. We were even taught to quilt by hand.

For me, there is something therapeutic, and yes, magical about cutting up lots of large and small pieces of cotton fabric, arranging them in a completely new way, and then sewing them all back together. No, seriously. For me, quilting, like writing, is a hugely creative outlet. I was spending lots of time at home and needed something like that. I could learn to quilt at my own pace. I made lots of mistakes, eventually improved my skills, and, after a bunch of years, I was good at it. After Mimi was born, it was more difficult to get out of the house at night. Many years later, when Katie and Ricky slowly left the nest to attend college and then marry, I spent way too much time at home hanging out with Mimi. So, when Mimi went to bed, I would work on a quilt project. Back then, I only completed a couple of quilts a year. After Katie and Ricky moved away, I was cranking out three or four a year. Most years, I still donate one quilt to charity, gift a couple, and keep one for myself. Over the years, I have made many quilts for the Village Learning Center's yearly gala, and even one for the MD Anderson Cancer Center's Ovarian Cancer Quilt Project. I have also participated in the making of many, many quilts for our church's Prayer Quilt Ministry.

—

I have volunteered for much of Mimi's life in the wacky world of special needs. I started as a room mother in her early childhood class. Later, I joined a parent group in the Humble Independent School District. I soon learned that special education, like all industries, has its own set of acronyms. We had a school district facilitator who tried his darnedest to guide us the best he could. Looking back, I feel certain it was more like herding cats. Getting a group of ladies to focus was not easy. Our little group met once a month during the school year. I was a member for at least ten years. Maybe more. Volunteering in that group was the smartest thing I did for myself and for Mimi. I desperately needed to connect to people who had children with special needs.

That first parent meeting began with maybe eight or nine or perhaps ten mothers sitting in a large circle. One at a time, we introduced ourselves and said something about our special child. I remember one of the mothers described her child as a "high-functioning, autistic teenager with suicidal tendencies." Those were her exact words. She told us how he was locked in his room each night so he wouldn't come in contact with sharp objects in other parts of the house. The mother was in constant fear her son would hurt himself or a family member.

When it was my turn to speak, I let everyone know my daughter was born with cerebral palsy, was mentally two years old, couldn't walk, read, or write, and was basically nonverbal.

After the parent meeting, several of the mothers went to lunch. I sat next to the mom with the autistic teenager.

"I wouldn't have your child for a million dollars," we said to each other at the same time.

I found her statement incredibly unexpected. To me, her son would be so difficult to care for. My child was easy. I wondered what I had said that sounded so difficult to deal with. Do we get used to the child God entrusted us with? Although to me it seemed unthinkable to have a suicidal teenager as my child, this mother wouldn't have it any other way. She loved her son deeply, as I loved my little Mimi.

In the beginning, I think it took our group a whole school semester to just figure out our mission statement. It is a wonder the facilitator didn't give up on us. We tended to get off on tangents some months. I often wondered if I was wasting my time. After the mission statement was finally hammered out, we started a school district newsletter for parents who had children with special needs. Our group wrote it, stapled it, and put the mailing labels on each one. The school district paid for the postage. Did I mention I was the editor and typed the newsletter? I had lots of help from fellow group members when it came to submitting articles. The newsletter went out a couple of times a year to parents whose children received any kind of special services.

I was amazed the first time we assembled the newsletter at how many children received services. There were hundreds of newsletters. The pages of labels were divided by school campuses. That was when I learned there were students receiving special services on every campus in the district. I also realized that most children probably had hidden challenges, like learning disabilities and speech issues. I feel certain that when most of us enter a school, it doesn't register for us that anyone on that campus has special needs. Mimi's cerebral palsy was so obvious. I had thought all special needs children were a lot like Mimi. I was totally wrong.

—

I met Kathie almost thirty years ago after Mass one Sunday. Her son, Nick, was born with Down syndrome, which totally does not define him. Down syndrome is a genetic disorder caused when abnormal cell division results in extra genetic material from chromosome 21. Delayed development and learning disabilities are associated with Down syndrome. Nick and our Ricky were in Cub Scouts together. Kathie and I worked on lots of special projects together over the years. I like to think of her as the "idea" person. I went along for the ride, helping to execute whatever project we were working on. Mimi and Nick were at Deerwood Elementary together for several years. Different classrooms, same school.

One year, Kathie and I joined the Deerwood PTA and created a Special Populations group. We started a curriculum called "Everybody Counts" that teaches elementary-age students about disabilities with hands-on activities. We wanted to teach the students that kids with special needs were more like them and not to be feared. As we soon learned, a little bit of understanding goes a long way.

The lessons were sensitive to the students' ages. I volunteered to teach children in one of the lower grades about what it was like to be blind. That was illuminating. At the start of the lesson, I recall first asking the class what they thought being blind was like. One of the kids raised her hand

and said it was like when her grandpa took off his glasses. He couldn't see. The lesson was as much for me as for the students. I was blown away by how the word "blind" had been misinterpreted. Then, I handed each child a paper mask held on with elastic and turned off the lights. I asked the students what they saw. Several said it was dark and they couldn't see anything. After turning on the lights, I asked them to remove their masks. Next, I told them that complete darkness was what being blind was like. I recall there was complete silence for a few moments following my statement.

I believe "Everybody Counts" is still taught at the elementary level at many schools in the district. This simple program has taught many hundreds of students to look at disabilities differently.

—

It was well over twenty years ago that Kathie and I approached the manager at our local YMCA. We had an idea! At the time, the Y had a program called Kids' Night Out for area children. For a small fee, when the Y closed on a Saturday evening, kids took over the place and had a great time. There were minimal volunteers. It allowed parents to have a few hours to go out for dinner or a movie.

Our school district parent group floated the idea of having a kids' night out for our children with special needs. The reasoning was twofold. First, children with special needs didn't have many social outlets. In many cases, they went to school, maybe church on Sunday, and came home. I saw it firsthand in our own home. Our Katie had lots of friends, was invited to birthday parties, went to sleepovers, had after-school activities, etc. Mimi, not so much. The YMCA program could give Mimi the opportunity to socialize.

It would also provide parents with a way to reconnect. They would have a few hours once a month to go out to dinner, or maybe a movie. In our case, Rick and I often just went to the grocery store together. Sounds lame, but it was kind of romantic. We lingered in the wine department.

Of course, our YMCA idea would require lots of supervision. But we thought teenager groups from local churches and the high school would love the volunteer hours. We couldn't believe it when the Y said yes to our proposal.

Before each event, the teens had an orientation and learned the rules. There needed to be a level of understanding that the teens would be buddies to our kids with special needs. If the teens had any questions during the event, a couple of parents were there to answer them. The YMCA provided a few staff, and there were parents from our parent group who were walking around facilitating.

Eventually, we added a Christmas party each December, a tradition that lasted for many years. A local church choir came and sang Christmas carols, there was a DJ and a dance, and kids enjoyed face painting, cookies, and drinks. The highlight for many, especially Mimi, was when Santa stopped by — and not just to mingle. There were photos with Santa. A local photographer took and donated the photos. There were multiple jolly gentlemen over the years who owned Santa suits and filled in as our Santa. It always amazed me how a few parents, volunteers, and a generous community could come together and create such an amazing event.

The YMCA program was a huge success, lasting just over twenty years, until Hurricane Harvey hit in 2017 and flooded the YMCA. But the seed we planted grew and bore so much fruit. The teen groups that volunteered came to naturally realize our kids with special needs were not so different from them.

I believe what this little night accomplished was more than just a place for those with special needs to hang out. The biggest impact was the way it changed the hearts of so many "normal" teenagers. They came back to volunteer month after month. Our daughter, Katie, volunteered for many years. These volunteers saw our special kids as kids first.

One year, I made a large wall quilt for the YMCA to thank them in some small way for hosting the Special Kids' Night Out. The background of the quilt was light blue with bold lettering and a large red heart. It hung for many years in one of the YMCA's hallways. The quilt had "Special Kids 'heart' YMCA" appliqued to the front of it. Just like the entire YMCA building complex and everything in it, the quilt was ruined when Hurricane Harvey flooded the YMCA.

Anecdotally, I was often reminded of the positive effects of the YMCA's Special Kids' Night Out. There were many times when Mimi and I were walking around the mall and a teenager would approach us. She would say hello to Mimi and reach out to give her a hug. Of course, I didn't know who they were. I had only met the buddies for a few minutes each month when Mimi was dropped off. Mimi had many, many YMCA buddies over the years. When I asked how she or he knew Mimi, it was always something like, "Oh, I was her buddy at Kids' Night Out. We had so much fun."

—

In the waning years of my participation in the parent group on the school district level, we had a parent who posed a question most of us dared not address. It was Kim who asked, "What will happen to our kids when they age out of school?" The answer was obvious. We all knew. It always went something like, "They will stay home with mom for the rest of their lives, mostly sitting in front of the television."

This was a depressing reality on so many levels. We had kids who loved going to school, and when it abruptly ended with high school graduation, that was it. For most, there would be no jobs, no college, no getting married, heck—not even a driver's license. Still, we loved our kids and wanted them to live to their potential. On a personal level, it has always been a difficult question to answer: where does Mimi fit in the world? My usual answer was right here in our home and in our community. Outside of that, I struggled with a realistic and comforting answer.

Then, there was the really tough question: "what will happen to our kids when we die?" That was the most difficult question of all. Rick and I had kicked that rusty tin can with muck in the bottom of it down the road many times.

Kim challenged us to make some road trips together to figure out what was out there. One visit was downtown to an institution/workshop. It was so depressing that I couldn't imagine any of our kids ever living there. Everyone was so old. It was like a nursing home for those with special needs. Our kids were on the cusp of aging out of school, not ready for a nursing-home environment.

We soon found out there weren't any day centers for those with intellectual disabilities anywhere near our area. This was a challenge that clearly needed a solution.

We had always thought it best for our kids to live in their own community, where they were loved and valued, with support. Kim and another mom stepped up and founded the Village Learning & Achievement Center. But that chapter is for later!

Chapter Three

So Much to Learn

*Never discourage anyone who continually
makes progress, no matter how slow.*

– Plato

I learned a new word when Mimi entered public school: diagnostician. To be more precise, it is a title. Before Mimi required one, I had never heard of a diagnostician. I soon learned it was the person we had to start with in order to enroll Mimi in special education in the school district. A diagnostician is commonly referred to as a learning consultant, and they often hold a master's in special education. The diagnostician is part of a team that will assess, diagnose, and treat children who are struggling with learning delays.

Our little family had moved back to Texas from Michigan. Mimi was now three years old and eligible for an early childhood program in the school district. The Michigan early intervention program for ages zero to three was set up for the same purpose. The goal in early childhood is for the child to hopefully catch up to their peers by the time he or she reaches kindergarten.

Mimi's special services program was determined after all the testing was complete and a plan put in place. Then an ARD (which stands for "admission, review, and dismissal") meeting was convened with the parents, diagnostician, teacher, and therapists. I am not certain if the ARD is a standard acronym in all states. Basically, we sat in a conference room and talked about the testing results and Mimi's plan for the school year, and signed paperwork — lots of paperwork. After that, ARD meetings generally were convened once a year.

But back to the diagnostician. In a peanut shell, the diagnostician orchestrated the testing to see what kinds of services Mimi would receive in public school. Several domains were tested, like social, fine motor, gross motor, and speech areas. I participated in the process by answering a list of questions on behalf of Mimi since she was nonverbal. Interestingly, we learned Mimi was very social but had deficits in the remainder of the domains.

Mimi's life skills program was at one of the elementary schools a few miles from our home. It was not our home campus — the one that Katie, and later Ricky, would attend two blocks away. Mimi also received transportation in one of those little buses with a wheelchair lift to and from school. I learned the number of students in Mimi's classroom would be small: four, five, or six at the most. The teacher would also have a classroom aide. Mimi would be learning within what the school district called a life skills program.

An IEP is an "individualized education plan." Each educational professional that worked with Mimi, like the teacher and multiple therapists, developed their own IEPs for the work they would do with Mimi during a school year. Parents have input as to whether they believe the activities are realistic. During each grading period, the teachers and therapists report their progress on the IEPs they are responsible for. It is nothing like a traditional report card. No As, Bs, or Cs. The goal is for an activity/learning skill to be "mastered." For example, one IEP entry from middle school reads, "Mimi will learn to drink from a straw."

I have known many diagnosticians over the years. Most were very professional and helpful. Of course, people always remember the one that was challenging, don't they?

—

There was this lady with short, spiky white hair and long fake finger-nails from a box, which were, way back in the '80s, not so much a fashion statement. I recall how this lady liked to tap them on the desk. Paired with the distracted look on her face, it seemed to be her way of saying she was impatient, and to hurry up.

My first meeting with the fake fingernail lady was her trying to convince me that Mimi needed to have an additional label — mentally retarded. Up until that time, Mimi had plenty of labels to qualify for special services. There was orthopedically handicapped, speech impaired, and other health impairments. The possibility of adding this new label was something Rick and I had already talked about at home. The mentally retarded label was not one we were comfortable with. We were not budging. We felt once a child had the label, it would never go away. Maybe we were wrong. But that is how we felt. We believed teachers and therapists might develop a preconceived notion of who Mimi was intellectually. Also, we did not feel it was necessary so early in elementary school to add such a label. Mimi was four years old.

The challenge with Mimi was her inability to communicate. The diagnostician agreed there was not one test that could accurately measure Mimi's intellectual level. Everyone agreed Mimi had some understanding that could not be communicated in a test. Mimi's difficulty with coordinating her hands and eyes did not allow her to point at pictures with accuracy or use a form of talking device.

Rather than sign off on the diagnostician's paperwork to add the label to Mimi in our meeting, I instead indicated we needed to talk further about this issue. I would be bringing my husband to our next meeting.

True to form, the fake fingernail lady was ready for us with a new nail color. We met in her small office a week or so later. Her sales pitch, including nail tapping, centered on informing us we would be doing Mimi a disservice if we did not add the MR (mentally retarded) label. If Mimi did not acquire the MR label, there were services she would not be entitled to as an adult. Of course, we told her all the reasons we didn't believe it was appropriate at that particular moment.

We asked her if she had tested Mimi. How exactly did she test our daughter, and could we see what IQ number she came up with? Was Mimi mildly, moderately, or severely retarded? Our questions were answered only with nail tapping. I certainly did not have any confidence in this lady testing Mimi. After a heated exchange, there was no way we were going to allow her to quantify Mimi's IQ. To say Rick and the diagnostician raised their voices was an understatement. Rick and I left the meeting disgusted. Mimi did not have the label added to her file. Maybe Mimi would eventually require the label. But it certainly was not necessary now. We would give her a chance to see how far she would go intellectually and then we would decide.

———

After our heated meeting, I agreed to bring Rick only to what we called "difficult ARD" meetings. These were the ARDs where someone in the room was trying to deny services or insist on something we did not agree with. It is not like I couldn't handle the ARDs myself, but sometimes it helps to have backup. Usually, these meetings have a conference room table filled with school professionals and only one parent. By the ARD meeting's very nature, a parent can feel intimidated. It was helpful when I accidently learned ARD meetings could be "tabled," or postponed, until another day. Sometimes facts would have to be gathered. Hasty decisions were not in my nature.

Some years I dreaded walking into an ARD meeting. It is not the fault of the school district. I just never liked the way they made me feel. All the parties went around the table talking about Mimi's strengths, but also her many weaknesses. Hearing about all the things she couldn't do brought up so many raw feelings. It was like each year we were talking about the day she started public school when she was three years old. I had moved way past that day and didn't care to relive it every year. I could feel my face redden and anxiety build in my insides. Some years, I would want to cry, but held it down deep in my gut. I never understood the purpose of reading out loud all the things she couldn't do. But I had done my homework and worked with the individuals around the table to get the best written IEPs for Mimi. I was there to advocate for Mimi.

Part of Mimi's IEP included time during the school day for physical, occupational, and speech therapy. Therapists are some of the most creative people I have ever encountered. They are required to find countless new ways to introduce the same skill to make it interesting and relevant. These therapies consisted of lots of repetition for one simple important movement. Over a long period of time, Mimi would conquer a skill and move on to the next. Some skills she never learned. Mimi had challenges eating, speaking, and with physical strength and balance. She had issues with hand-eye coordination.

Mimi didn't learn much on her own and needed lots of encouragement. Most years she interacted with more adults, such as teachers, aides, bus drivers, and therapists, than with her student peers. Many of the students in her class were virtually nonverbal, so how could she relate to them? I wouldn't have believed it unless I lived it right beside her! Yet through all the challenges, Mimi remained joyful, funny, social, spiritual, and adorable.

—

Physical therapy, or PT, was an interesting world. Early on there was always the possibility that Mimi would be able to walk. We worked so hard toward making that a reality. During school hours, Mimi was pulled out of class for one-on-one physical therapy. The physical therapist, or PT, also worked in Mimi's classroom with the teacher on ideas for proper seating, etc. The PT assisted the teacher with any techniques they could employ during the school day to further her PT goals. I also was able to collaborate with the PT and use some of her creative methods at home. With the help of Mimi's PT, we started to accumulate special seating and bathing equipment to accommodate Mimi.

I am not certain when Mimi learned to manipulate the physical therapist. I do remember the day I got a call from the PT to see if I would meet with her at school. She was having an issue during her last few one-on-one sessions with Mimi. I arrived at the school right before Mimi was pulled out and just stood back and watched so I could get a feel for what was going on.

About a minute into her therapy, Mimi flashed the sign language sign for "potty," along with a concerned look. Mimi had learned this sign early — about the same time as her colors. The sign for "I need to go potty" is basically to make a fist with one hand and then shake it to and fro. The therapist told me the potty sign was happening regularly. First the sign, and, if the PT didn't stop working with Mimi, a very concerned "Mimi sad face" emerged. Then a very vigorous potty sign was employed.

Because the PT didn't want to ignore the possibility Mimi needed to use the potty, she stopped the therapy session. She would then move to the bathroom, and Mimi would sit like a happy princess holding court for the rest of the session. And Mimi did not go potty. She just didn't want to participate in physical therapy activities. Yep, Mimi had learned to effectively control through manipulation. I confirmed it. Our daughter was a lot like our other two children in the way they manipulated. We adults had to be smarter.

In elementary school, part of Mimi's physical therapy regimen was to "stand" in a stander for a short period of time. A stander is a large piece of equipment that supports the trunk of the body and hips. It helped her bear weight on her feet. There was a tray attached so Mimi could perform little activities instead of just standing there until her confinement was over. It took a couple of people to get Mimi strapped into the stander. In the beginning, I received notes that she was tolerating it very well.

Then one day I happened to stop by the classroom for some reason. It was definitely divine intervention. I am convinced Mimi's guardian angel made me leave something out of her backpack that morning.

Upon entering the classroom, I noticed Mimi was not in the room. The teacher indicated she was with the physical therapist across the hall. As I opened the door to where Mimi and the therapist were, I heard sobbing. There was Mimi in the stander bellowing, with large tears running down her face. The therapist did not look alarmed and came over to me. She explained that Mimi had been sobbing for a couple of weeks while in the stander. It was why they were not in her classroom while standing. Obviously, the class would be upset. It was the therapist's opinion Mimi was manipulating them, like she had done with the potty sign. This was a different physical therapist. It was clear she knew something about Mimi's manipulative abilities. I questioned if maybe the stander was painful for Mimi.

"Let's get her out of the stander and talk about what is going on," I said, with an urgency in my voice.

As we were loosening the Velcro straps holding Mimi in the stander, I noticed a thick shim under one of her feet. The PT explained it was to square up her hips so Mimi could stand equally flat on the left and right side of her body.

It is difficult to explain the state of Mimi's hips. One side of her body pulled one way and the other side pulled another. Cerebral palsy caused her muscles and tendons to be tight but to different degrees, which caused distortions. Several years later, while Mimi sat in a wheelchair, one hip pulled forward, making it appear as if one of her legs were longer than the other.

In my mind, there were two issues with the stander. First the screaming and then the shim. I had not been informed of the sobbing or the shim. How could this happen, and I not know? I felt there was a disconnect between the school and me. A simple note in Mimi's spiral notebook by her teacher, or the PT, would have raised a call to action. I was hugely disappointed no one thought to inform me about Mimi and the stander. There was a meeting at school about the stander and it was discontinued. Clearly, it was indeed painful to Mimi.

A few words about the spiral notebook. Each year, I purchased a new notebook (college ruled) and had Mimi's name printed large on the front cover in black permanent marker. The notebook was placed in Mimi's wheelchair backpack. I always started off the first day of school with contact information and chatty thoughts about Mimi. I invited back-and-forth communication. Some school years, I purchased two notebooks because of extra-chatty teachers. The notebook was the first thing I checked after school while Mimi was eating her after-school snack. It was a lifeline for me to figure out what happened at school each day.

It was always my prayer at the beginning of a new school year for Mimi to have a teacher who would be a great communicator. The notebook helped me let the teacher peek into our little window at home. I hoped the daily tidbits would help the teacher understand our quiet daughter.

I told the teachers stories about what happened at home. Things like what Mimi ate for dinner, how we walked around the block, ran into neighbors, and visited. If we went out as a family to eat, I let them know what Mimi ate. If we went to a movie, the teacher got an earful about how much Mimi liked the movie and the popcorn. By middle school, her gag reflex evened out with most foods. As long as she was able to wash the residual popcorn down with a little Coca-Cola, Mimi was a happy camper.

I have stacks of spiral notebooks with daily "conversations" between Mimi's teachers and me. It started during her early childhood years and continued right through high school. How else do you figure out what happened at school all day? Mimi could not tell me — ever.

After the incident with Mimi crying in the stander in middle school, I learned to show up randomly to really know what was going on in the classroom. Obviously, some important details were not coming home in the spiral notebook.

—

Mimi also received occupational therapy (OT) during the school day. OT mostly has to do with fine motor control like writing, manipulating things, eating, drinking, etc.

Mimi's greatest challenge with her fine motor control was using her frail little hands. Imagine not being able to sign your name your whole life because your fingers and hands would not allow it. The best we got from Mimi was a little scribble with a crayon with her left hand. I don't believe working with her hands was painful. There was never a look of pain on her face. It was more like intense concentration trying to make those fingers work for a few seconds — and she was done. At one point, we even tried to teach Mimi to use a rubber stamp to "sign" her name. It was a nice try, but it didn't work.

There were other fine motor skills that were delayed in Mimi's life. Babies typically learn the pincer grasp between eight and twelve months of age. This is the skill where the thumb and index finger are used together to manipulate small objects, like picking up a single Cheerio. Mimi was in late elementary school when she finally mastered this skill, but only in her left hand. I used to tease the occupational therapist that she was responsible for the skill that taught Mimi how to pinch people. A delicate pinch from Mimi to her mom's arm was her favorite way to use a pincer grasp. Afterwards, Mimi would squeal in delight.

And don't get me started on sipping from a straw. Whenever I see a little child sipping a drink from a straw, I am still in awe. I sometimes wonder if the mother knows what a grand gift simply being able to sip from a straw is. Just think for a moment about all the skill involved in wrapping your lips around a simple straw and sucking in so that liquid will draw up the straw and finally land into the mouth. Then being able to hold the liquid for a wee moment in your mouth and swallow.

Alas, it was not to be for Mimi. This one skill was on her IEP for several years. There was a moment in an ARD meeting in high school when I told the OT to just take it off and move on to something that might be just as meaningful, and hopefully attainable. She never learned to drink from a child's sippy cup. It was too difficult as well. But Mimi could hold a cup with her left hand, drink from a cup filled halfway, and then place the cup down without spilling. I was only too happy to live with her drinking from a cup.

Like physical therapists, occupational therapists often work in the classroom with the teacher, coming up with different activities to promote the same or similar goals for Mimi, like feeding herself, stacking blocks, putting a coin in a slot, and so much more.

Mimi being able to feed herself was a major skill that took lots of practice. She learned to scoop with a spoon in her left hand. It was stunning how that little left hand could scoop up cut-up pieces of pancakes from a low-rimmed bowl so perfectly. I would marvel during breakfast at how Mimi would slowly maneuver her spoon and chase the final piece of pancake onto her spoon and into her mouth.

We modified her meal on the plate when we ate out at a restaurant so Mimi would be successful eating by herself in public. If we were eating at a Tex-Mex restaurant, I mixed up refried beans and rice. It was perfect. Or if eating at Luby's, a cafeteria-style sit-down restaurant, I always chose mashed potatoes with chicken and a veggie. It only took a few minutes to cut up the chicken and vegetables and mix it into the mashed potatoes. It was one of her favorite meals. Mimi never mastered stabbing food with a fork, or using a knife, but that was fine. There were certain things she could finger-feed herself, like a peanut butter and jelly sandwich or grilled cheese cut in quarters. And don't get me started on French fries. Once the pincer grasp kicked in, she could handle French fries just fine. They were her favorite.

Mimi learning to stack blocks was an interesting thing to watch. This is something small children learn way before they even hit preschool. We also worked on this skill at home. Unfortunately, Mimi was still working on stacking well into elementary school. Again, eyes and hands cooperating at the same time is a must. I don't believe Mimi ever managed to stack more than three blocks. It was something she could never do easily.

I recall that while taking a college class, I received permission to photograph Mimi at school. One of the black-and-white photographs for my final college project was all about Mimi placing a coin into a slot. I made an appointment to watch Mimi work with her teacher on this skill so I could photograph it. The teacher told me they started with a quarter because it was large, and they made the slot larger to make it easy. Eventually, as the skill was mastered, they would use a penny with a smaller slot. The level of concentration on Mimi's part was intense. I saw just how difficult it was for her to force those big blue eyes to look at the slot and move the coin in her hand over it and then drop it. It took several tries. But when the coin dropped through the slot, Mimi was so proud of herself, letting out a "yeah" and clapping.

—

Speech therapy was another area where Mimi challenged her therapists. Early sign language words like "cow" (think about using two hands to milk a cow), "potty" (shaking your fist), "more," "crackers," "elephant," and "monkey" are standard signs she learned. Mimi also learned the signs for basic colors. Much later, when her speech, although limited, emerged, Mimi could verbally "say" her colors, but would also sign them at the same time.

However, her first response to the question "What color is this?" was usually "blue." I always thought surely blue had to be her favorite color. I believe it was more like her pat answer. Mimi was eager to please. It was the one answer she could give, and then the teacher, or Mommy, might move on to some more fun activity. However, when she was given a second chance at naming the color, it was usually the correct choice.

Mimi's signing was not perfect. Since her little fingers and hands did not work well, the signing was a bit messy. If you were around her enough, you knew what she meant. I taught her the sign for "gray." I believe it was from a Sesame Street book on sign language. It is one of my proudest mommy moments that will go down in signing history.

Along the way, the speech therapists worked with Mimi using all kinds of techniques, from advanced technology (at the time) to plain old finger pointing at pictures. Again, the challenge for Mimi was the hand-eye coordination. If you asked her to point at a picture of a ball, she had great difficulty taking her finger and pointing it at the ball. Her eyes and fingers just couldn't make that connection. It is the reason technology didn't work for Mimi. She had lots of kiddie books at home with buttons to push that made sounds. She loved pushing them. But if you asked her to push a certain button, she could not.

The limited sign language did help. She eventually gained some speech, although it was more like one- and two-word phrases. One time, while she was attending middle school, I wrote down every word Mimi could verbalize. It amounted to about two hundred words. She knew more people's names than she did actual things. That is a testament to her being so social. Her favorite signing words were "pancakes" and "outside."

Mimi could not enunciate her full first name. I reasoned "Melanie" had way too many syllables. Try saying it out loud three times real fast. See what I mean? Your tongue twists a little in your mouth. Our little Ricky had one heck of a time with it. He was probably two or so when he started calling his sister "Mimi," and it stuck. Mimi was probably five when she started introducing herself by lightly tapping her chest and saying "I'm Mimi" to everyone. She has been Mimi ever since.

There are many ways to speak: words, signs, body language, a smile, and a great big Mimi hug. I learned to pay attention to the little things, and hoped I was getting it right.

—

Part of Mimi's world during school also involved community-based instruction, or, in public school lingo, CBI. There were lots of instructional and social outings to the grocery story, the public library — basically any place where learning life skills happens in a real way. For instance, her class might make a shopping list and then head to the grocery store to find the ingredients for a recipe to be made later at school.

Mimi and her middle and high school classes also went out into the world to learn things in a community setting. One of her favorite social outings was bowling. Bowling was a CBI beloved by the life skills crowd. Of course, knocking down a bunch of bowling pins was the point, but it was so fun. I feel certain no one cared much about who had the highest score.

Some of the skills learned were taking turns, patience, and good sportsmanship. During the early years, Mimi used to push a bowling ball from a plastic kiddie slide. By the time she reached middle school, the bowling alleys acquired ramps that were much safer.

After years of PT, OT, and speech therapy in public school, Mimi was making progress. While she never learned to walk, her manual wheelchair took her lots of places. She could feed herself with some assistance, turn the pages of a book, stack a few blocks, communicate simple desires, play catch with a ball, make friends, pinch her mom, talk in one- and two-word phrases, and love fiercely via hugs.

I was amazed that she never stopped learning. I credit her adult day center, the Village Learning & Achievement Center, as a huge factor in her continuing to learn new words and advance her understanding. The staff really challenged Mimi.

—

In 2007, when Mimi was twenty-three years old, I wrote a column for *The Tribune* newspaper about Mimi learning a new word. Words with more than two syllables spoken by Mimi were a rarity. Throughout her life, she continued to add words to her vocabulary. Each was a victory and contributed to my understanding of her.

The Tribune
You Gotta Laugh —
"Anyway You Say It … Dorable Is Still Adorable"
Written by Dixie Frantz
Published April 11, 2007

My handicapped daughter learned a brand-new word last week. We were watching some television show together and one of the actors on the old boob tube uttered the word "adorable." Mimi looked at me kinda puzzled, and promptly said, "dorable." My eyebrows immediately lurched skyward. Not since the early days of speech therapy in public school had I heard a new word, let alone one with so many syllables.

Now the young lady perched in her wheelchair only speaks in one-and-two-word phrases, with a total vocabulary of about two hundred words. I know because I counted them once. Some of her spoken words might lack a beginning, or an ending, but everyone in the family knows exactly what she is talkin' about.

"It means beautiful," I answered.

"Oh," Mimi shot back, with a thoughtful look on her face.

The word must have left a major impression because she has probably used it three thousand times since our little conversation. Pretty much everything is "dorable." Vanna on the Wheel of Fortune is definitely "dorable." The large red-headed woodpecker hanging upside down off the bird feeder in the backyard is "dorable." Oh, and the lioness about to take a chunk out of the back side of the water buffalo on the National Geographic Channel is "dorable." Not to worry … I changed the channel before the razor-sharp teeth made contact with said wild animal. And yeah, I realize I've got my work cut out for me after Mimi's "dorable" comment about the water buffalo/lioness confrontation.

Heck, even Mimi's dad is "dorable," though I always counter with, "No, your daddy is handsome." What can I say ... it's a mom's job to keep things real.

The true test will be when her little brother comes home from college for the summer in a couple of weeks. If Mimi connects the two words "dorable" and Ree-Ree (that's what Mimi calls her brother Ricky), I'll have hubby immediately dial 9-1-1. Yeah, because for certain, I'll be the one having the heart attack.

Mimi and Ricky's brother/sister relationship is a complicated one. Only three years separate the siblings, who many years ago shared a double umbrella stroller until Ricky grew too wide to fit his plump tush beside his extremely petite sister. When Mimi finally grew into a wheelchair stroller at about the age of five, Ricky took it upon himself to perch on the large foot ledge between Mimi's tiny feet during our frequent walks around the block. When Mimi had enough of her brother's incessant squirming, she would reach down and grab a handful of his hair and slowly yank his head back. Had to admit, the lad certainly tolerated her abuse well. Actually, Ricky could have cared less. For him it was all about the free ride.

I guess Mimi has always viewed her little brother as somewhat of an annoyance, even though he was the one who taught her to bang the pots and pans in mom's kitchen.

And when the lad was the one belching loudly at the dinner table, it was Mimi who promptly shot her little brother one of those melting steel glances from across the table before anyone could verbally correct the lad. Mimi learned her gracious manners at home and in the world of special education at school. Concepts like excuse me, please and thank you were always low on the totem pole of priorities for little brother.

"'Cuse me," Mimi would utter loudly for Ricky's sake after each of his flurry of belches.

Yep, and the girl has still got one squinty eye glued on her little brother. Over the Christmas holidays, she caught him drinking directly from the milk carton and nearly had a cow.

I have a sneaky feeling there will be no need to make that emergency 9-1-1 call when Ricky steps through the back door in a couple of weeks. Betcha nine dollars Mimi's little brother is nowhere near her long list of "dorable." Clearly, it is the water buffalo that wins that award.

Chapter Four

The Wheels on the Bus
Go Round and Round

All the world is full of suffering.
It is also full of overcoming.

— Helen Keller

School life for Mimi was so different than what I had experienced with our oldest child. First, Katie was five years old when she entered kindergarten, and it was a school right down the street from our house. Mimi was just three when she entered the doors of public school in a different neighborhood. I wasn't sure I was prepared for the world of special education, but I became a fast learner.

Mimi never went to her home school campus until high school. Mimi's life skills program was always at another school in the district. She started at the very tender age of three.

I understood why the school district grouped their special populations on different campuses. There were not many students like Mimi, and they did not all live in our little neighborhood.

There was a definite difference in how Mimi was perceived while visiting Katie's and Ricky's schools. For instance, when Mimi attended a school carnival at Katie's school, Mimi was sometimes looked at differently. Their school had a special population, but it was one of those invisible ones. Perhaps students were receiving speech therapy or special help with reading. It was nothing like the life skills program Mimi attended. Her special needs were as obvious as the wheelchair she used.

I remember sitting in the cafeteria with Mimi during the carnival, helping her with a snack. One young child looked at Mimi in horror. Her eyes were bulging, and her mouth was open. She got up out of her seat, taking great care to make a wide berth, avoiding Mimi while staring in her direction. The look on that child's face told me she thought Mimi was an alien from outer space. It suddenly became uncomfortable sitting in that room. I wanted to run with Mimi for the exit. But we stayed. We received a few similar stares throughout the day, only not as animated. It hurt a little, but I got it. When children are not exposed to those with special needs, they just do not know how to react.

We never received that response from the students where Mimi attended school. Kids at her school carnival tended to crowd around Mimi, waiting for their turn for a hug. Their parents looked on in awe. I think they wondered how a little girl in a wheelchair had affected so many kids. She could have had her own hug booth and charged lots of money. What a great school fundraiser idea!

Mimi's school had special education students in life skills and applied skills programs. Applied skills had higher-functioning students than life skills. These two populations also had the opportunity to be included in classes with the regular population. Magical things happen to those in life skills and applied skills programs when regular education children are the ones initiating tether ball on the playground or, in Mimi's case, helping her with her lunch. Relationships are forged and hearts are changed. It wasn't the fault of any of the kids at Katie's, and later, Ricky's school. It was a great elementary school. They just didn't have the opportunities that Mimi's school had with special needs students.

—

Mimi was just three years old the first time she rode a little yellow school bus with a wheelchair lift to her elementary school. I carried her onto the bus each day and strapped her into a car seat. She did not have a wheelchair until sometime later. Mimi weighed hardly more than a large sack of potatoes and had little bitty thin arms and spindly legs.

After saying my first brief hello and goodbye to the bus driver, I vividly remember standing at the end of the driveway that very first day. Tears streamed down my cheeks as the bus turned the corner. That first week was rough. Some parents are beyond happy and excited on their child's first day of school. I was terrified. It was an understatement to say I was growing right beside Mimi.

Mimi never had behavior issues. Well, there was this one time she threw her crayons in middle school, but that is another story. Unfortunately, Mimi could be very content just sitting back and watching. I knew that if she were not engaged by the teacher or staff, it would have a negative effect on her learning.

I can recall one school year being at a parent-teacher conference. The special education teacher was surprised when I mentioned Mimi could talk. It seems she wasn't saying anything in class. I told her maybe she should ask Mimi a question. She might be surprised. After that comment, I made it a point to write in the spiral notebook about the little conversations Mimi and I would have each day. It might be just one- and two-word phrases coming out of her mouth, but they were clearly words. By this time, she was calling me "Mommy." Her dad was "Daddy." Her sister, Katie, was lovingly "Tadie," and her little brother, Ricky, was "Re-Re." Oh, and our dog Peaches was "Pee-Wee." Not sure how that name evolved, but she sure loved that dog. Mimi said it with so much emotion. Mimi would say "Pee-Wee," cock her head to one side, raise her shoulders as if to make them meet, and then sigh "awwww."

Some school years I went through several notebooks if a teacher was chatty. Obviously, I knew it took time out of a busy teacher's schedule. I mean, let's face it, you can't have a parent-teacher conference once a week.

Even as an adult, Mimi never learned to tell me what happened at school or at the adult day center. She lived in the present and always looked forward to what was going to happen in the immediate next moment. Most every day when I retrieved her from the bus at the end of the day, she wouldn't be off the wheelchair lift yet and would already be asking to go to "Donald's" (McDonald's) or the mall. But there were lots of days I didn't have a clue what happened while Mimi was at school. Communication is so important. It was a constant effort to figure out how to effectively communicate with and about Mimi. Everyone needs to be heard and understood — especially those who cannot communicate.

—

There was an early childhood class across the hall from Mimi's life skills program. They didn't have the challenges the kids in Mimi's class had. All of them could walk, and there were a lot of students talking in this lively class.

I recall having a conversation in the school hallway with the teacher, Ms. Susie, about her class of cute little students. She casually mentioned not one of them was potty-trained. This concerned her greatly, and she immediately decided it would be her primary focus. Each of the students would be potty-trained by the end of the semester. All of them! This was a lady on a mission. Ms. Susie used M&M's as her reward system, and darn if she didn't have all those kids potty-trained in no time. I had a great deal of respect for her. She knew this was a crucial skill for each of her little students.

Speaking as a mother who never gave up on potty-training Mimi her whole life, I totally got it. If the Blessed Mother had come to me in a dream and granted me one wish for Mimi, it would have been for her to be potty-trained. It never happened. The Blessed Mother had other plans for Mimi.

I can't say early childhood was easy for Mimi ... or for me. I think there were five or six tiny students with varying disabilities in her class. The young teacher and aide were lovely, caring ladies, and so creative. I could tell the social interaction was stimulating for Mimi, even though the whole class was pretty much nonverbal. Mimi loved the little preschool songs. There was also lots to learn: emergency signs, simple sign language, and other such things. Mimi was pulled out of the classroom at various times so she could receive such services as speech, occupational, and physical therapies.

—

I did have a run-in with Mimi's teacher about her learning to drink from a cup. Up until that point, Mimi received her fluids, such as milk and apple juice, through a baby bottle. She just could not get the hang of drinking from a regular cup, any type of child's sippy cup, or, God forbid, a straw. I don't know what it was about getting those little lips of hers to connect to a cup, but it was just not happening with any of these alternatives. But it was amazing to watch how she could suck fluids out of a bottle. Of course, this did not go well at school.

It wasn't long into the school year when her teacher started writing me notes like "Don't send Mimi baby bottles to school. She will not be using them. They are forbidden, we're not doing it, etc. I worried every day that Mimi would surely dehydrate into a pile of dust on the floor, as she was not getting any fluids while in school. That was a lot of hours! The exact moment she arrived home, I fed her a bottle of milk, which she nearly sucked inside out. I could tell by her dry and cracked lips she was thirsty, even though she could not tell me. It was a very tense time.

I didn't know who was going to crack first — me or Mimi. After a little conference, I knew for certain it would not be the teacher. All these years later, I can't tell you how long this went on. I feel certain I have blocked out the unpleasant memory. It could have been a couple of weeks, or maybe much longer. But suddenly, one day, Mimi got the hang of drinking from a cup. Mt. Everest was most certainly climbed that day, and I gladly placed the baby bottles into the trash.

I was often conflicted about what was best for Mimi, especially with the baby bottle vs. cup issue. Intellectually, I knew it was not appropriate for a five-year-old to drink from a bottle. But where was the line in the sand between harming her by taking it completely away and helping her? It was a difficult line to pole vault over. I think every parent has a moment like this with raising their children.

—

For one year, Mimi's early childhood program moved to Hidden Hollow Elementary School. I think Mimi was four years old, but maybe closer to five because of her summer birthday. I was one of the moms who volunteered to be a room mother. I assisted with class parties and a special project. It also afforded me the opportunity to see Mimi in a classroom setting and perhaps assist the teacher and aide in understanding our non-verbal daughter.

Hidden Hollow had a tradition back then that all the classes were to make a quilt that would be auctioned. It was a fundraiser that was attached to an event. Mimi's teacher and aide decided it would be fun to make a painted handprint quilt. I loved the idea. Each muslin fabric block had a student's handprints and name. There would also be a block for the teacher and classroom aide on the quilt. I assisted with the project and sewed the squares together, layered them with fluffy batting and backing fabric, did some simple machine quilting, and sewed on the binding. It was a lovely wall hanging. Of course, when it came time to auction the quilt, I had to purchase it. Sewing those squares connected me to this special quilt. It hung in Mimi's room for years.

Each set of handprints on the quilt was unique. They told a story that reflected the child's disability. Mimi's were the smallest of all the students. Tiny, thin, straight fingers that didn't work very well. Yep — her hands had cerebral palsy written all over them!

Then there was the little girl born with Rett syndrome, a rare genetic neurological disorder that occurs almost exclusively in girls. It leads to severe impairments, affecting nearly every aspect of a child's life, like their ability to speak, walk, eat, and even breathe easily. One characteristic of Rett syndrome is the almost constant repetitive hand movements, or shaking.

She was the most beautiful little thing you ever saw, with long dark hair and big brown eyes with long dark lashes. Her mother was lovely and dressed her daughter in frilly dresses, white-laced socks, and patent leather shoes. The little doll was nonverbal, and her hands shook terribly. I remember the teacher saying how difficult it was to get a good handprint from her. Looking at the muslin square, you can tell by the smudges that her hands were shaking on the quilt. I admired how the teachers took the time to get it right.

There was also a little boy who couldn't open one of his hands. I don't know the reason, but the teacher explained that after lots of thought they came up with a wonderful solution for the quilt. They applied paint to his right hand and printed it on the fabric twice, as if it were a right and left hand. That little boy grew leaps and bounds over Mimi. I remember seeing him many years later working at our local grocery store at the cash register.

I resisted saying to him as he was checking me out one time that I knew him when he was a little boy. I was thinking it though.

Another set of handprints that were striking were the chubby little handprints of Kelsie, born with Down syndrome. Mimi's and Kelsie's paths would cross many times over the decades. The little girl with the sweetest spirit would be on the same bus route some years, attend the same summer camp as Mimi some years, and at the end of Mimi's life she attended the same day center. Kelsie always called me "Mimi's Mom." Kelsie grew leaps and bounds past Mimi. She was such a dear, and clearly felt a deep connection to Mimi.

I saw Kelsie at a day center event some months after Mimi died. I had been invited to the Thanksgiving feast as a guest. I should not have gone. It was too soon. Kelsie was so sad when she came up to me at the event and just gave me a big hug. Buckets of tears flowed out of both of us. I left soon after. I don't think Kelsie understood the finality of death. I too still struggle with this, as I still feel Mimi in my heart.

The interesting thing about the handprint quilt was that these little children may have started out together in the early childhood program, but that certainly did not determine how far they would go in life. Several of the children would go on to hold jobs, like Kelsie. And then there was Mimi. She may have been perpetually stuck in the delightful world of a two-year-old intellectually, but she sprinkled her fairy dust of happiness and signature fierce hugs by the bucketful wherever she wandered.

Mimi attended elementary school for more years than the usual student. It was difficult to tie her to an actual grade. Children in the special education world start at age three and age out at twenty-two years old. That meant that somewhere along the way you might spend a few more years than most kids in elementary, middle, or high school. Mimi wasn't being held back, exactly. It was more like Mimi moved to the next level when she was good and ready, and age had little to do with it. Mimi spent eight years between early childhood and elementary school. Middle school was four years, with two years spent at the ninth-grade campus and the rest in high school. I believe it worked well for Mimi. She was moving through her school life in a way that worked best for her.

—

Some of Mimi's best years were spent at Deerwood Elementary School. It certainly had a wonderful principal with a loving attitude toward our special population. At the time Mimi was there, they had an applied skills and life skills program.

Mimi had been in attendance a couple of years when someone behind the scenes started talking about inclusion for the students in life skills and applied skills. I never knew who exactly planted the seed. I feel certain it would have been interesting to be a fly on the wall when they started talking about our Mimi. In what kind of regular education class do you put someone like her? Mimi barely talked. She was cute as a button, but a real mystery kid to the outside world if ever there was one.

By the time I had a meeting with Mimi's life skills teacher, I could tell it was all but decided. Mimi would attend homeroom with second graders. The more I thought about it, the more I liked the idea. Even at her tender age of five, I struggled with where Mimi fit in the world. It was a question my husband and I would ponder for her whole life. Mimi fit perfectly in our family, but beyond that, it was a challenge. Sure, homeroom wasn't math or science, which would not have been remotely appropriate, but it was a start. The main thing was Mimi would be in a classroom for part of the day with students who spoke.

The paperwork was signed in her annual ARD meeting in May. It was a done deal. Mimi would be attending homeroom in Mrs. Keeling's class in the fall. I was told Ms. Keeling was handpicked for the job and was excited for Mimi to be in her class. It was an easy sell for me. Who didn't want to have their child in a class with speaking students with a teacher who embraced them? Little did I know how this simple act of inclusion would impact Mimi's remaining years at Deerwood.

It was probably the second week of the new school year when I got a call from Mrs. Keeling. The homeroom students were asking Mrs. Keeling all kinds of questions about Mimi she could not answer. Things like, what did she like to do after school? What were her favorite shows to watch on television? She wondered if I would come to her class and answer the questions for Mimi. What an opportunity. I jumped in with both feet, not knowing what I was getting into.

Mrs. Keeling's class had close to twenty lively boys and girls squirming in their seats that morning. Mimi was sitting in her wheelchair at one side of the room when I got there. After Mrs. Keeling introduced me, little arms went up and great questions followed. Holding Mimi's little hand, I told them Mimi loved eating French fries, no ketchup, and chicken nuggets at McDonald's. She loved *Wheel of Fortune* on television. She loved bowling with her family, going to the movies, walking around the block with her mom, and she had a little brother and an older sister. The kids' eyes grew bigger with each question I answered. That day a whole classroom of kids learned Mimi wasn't a wheelchair with a kid in it. She was much like them. It was a game changer. Before I left the class for home, the kids crowded around Mimi and there were hugs all around.

As a result of my encounter in Mimi's new homeroom, interesting things started happening in her life. Some things you don't have to teach. I have said it before. Just give children an opportunity, stand back, and watch what happens. Empathy doesn't have to be taught when it is organically lived.

Near the end of the school year, I recall the time the second graders were going on their annual field trip to the Houston zoo. Mrs. Keeling indicated Mimi would also be going. She then asked if I would like to chaperone Mimi and a few kids from the class. She arranged for a wheelchair-accessible bus. I don't recall what happened at the zoo, but the bus trip down there was lively. I think there were three kids, Mimi, and myself along with the bus driver. The kids wanted to talk about Mimi. Puts a smile on my face whenever I think about those adorable little children.

—

A Mother's Day program at Deerwood Elementary inspired me to write a column about the experience in our local newspaper. In 2003, I submitted a slightly different version, which was published in a book of inspirational stories entitled *Chicken Soup for the Soul Celebrates Teachers*. Some things are so important you have to put them out there. It appears below.

Chicken Soup for the Soul Celebrates Teachers
"Mrs. Keeling's Class"
Written by Dixie Frantz
Published in 2003

A teacher did a number on my heartstrings with an "end of school year" gift when my daughter Mimi was in the second grade.

It was the first-year wheelchair-bound Mimi, a loveable child of very few words, was placed in a homeroom class with "normal" children. Even though she had attended the same elementary school for several years, Mimi had not had the opportunity to mingle much with regular education students.

Her homeroom teacher, Mrs. Keeling, made her an integral part of the classroom activities very naturally from the first day, and after a few weeks invited me to talk to the students. She called it a "teachable moment" since her students asked questions about Mimi that she couldn't answer. They asked me stuff like, "What does Mimi like to do for fun? What is she saying with her hands?"

Although our daughter is not deaf, her classmates learned that special needs children are often taught sign language to express themselves.

I called the moment a turning point in Mimi's life. I think for the first time her peers thought of her as a "kid in a wheelchair" instead of a "wheelchair with a kid in it."

It was a very good school year. Mimi started receiving little notes in her wheelchair backpack from a boy in her class named Joe, often with mazes for her to solve. Because Mimi couldn't read or write, I started sending him notes and signing them with Mimi's name. They often included little tidbits about what Mimi had done over the weekend. I think he knew who was really sending them, but Joe never let on. It wasn't until a couple of years later that I learned from his mother that Joe had been the new kid in class that year and was having a difficult time making friends.

The school year ended with a traditional second-grade program where children honor their mothers. The festivities ended with each student coming before the audience and announcing in a loud, clear voice, "I love my mother because ..." The student then found his or her mother in the audience and handed her a single flower.

I was sitting there with tears streaming down my cheeks, not only because it was so sweet, but silently grieving because Mimi would never be able to tell me with words why she loved me. At that moment in my life, I was probably between denial and acceptance over her disability, and that added to the emotion of the event.

As it turned out, Mimi was saved for last.

Mrs. Keeling wheeled her to the front and—in a very natural way— announced why Mimi loved her mother and then handed me a flower. I don't remember the exact words Mrs. Keeling spoke. I'm sure the renewed gush of tears must have affected my hearing. It was then I realized Mimi tells me many times every day why she loves me. She has simply replaced the words with two thin arms gripped tightly around my neck.

Over the next three years while Mimi attended the elementary school, I came to know many other wonderful young students who reached out to our daughter. They assisted her with lunch, helped her play tetherball on the playground and came into the special education room to play board games.

It wasn't long before everywhere our family went in the community, Mimi had a school buddy coming up to give her a hug.

My husband would often ask, "Who was that?" and I'd just smile and say, "I'm not sure about that one. Must be one of her friends from Mrs. Keeling's class."

—

Back in the late 1980s in Texas, none of the school buses, the little special education buses included, were equipped with air-conditioning. That might not have been a huge issue when school was out for the summer. But then, there was summer school, and the summers are hot and humid in the Houston area.

Lots of special education students receive services for a number of weeks through the summer. The idea is to not lose valuable skills learned during the school year. Since Mimi was always behind, naturally she went to summer school.

I noticed the temperatures in the mornings were not so bad when I helped the bus driver load Mimi on the bus. But the afternoons were just awful. Because of the location of the wheelchair lift, Mimi sat at the back of the bus. The driver had a fan at the front, but it soon became evident that little air reached the back of the bus. When I retrieved Mimi each afternoon, the poor little thing was one giant hot puddle. This could not go on. I didn't have a way to get her to school from home without assistance, or I would have taken her to and from summer school. I did consider not sending her to summer school at all.

For several years, I would call the school district and inquire if they were ever going to outfit their buses with air-conditioning. Most of the time I never heard back. A few times it was mentioned that it was not in the budget. I was also told none of the big buses had air-conditioning. That was true. But those students probably didn't go to summer school, weren't heat sensitive, on medications, or prone to seizures. In our parent group through the school district, we discussed it one time. A few other parents had expressed the same concern to the district with no reciprocal interest.

It wasn't until one parent joined our parent group that magic happened. Her name was Irish. I like to think of her as our little community organizer. She had a potential solution and called a meeting of interested parents to her home. There were about fifteen or twenty parents at this meeting. We went from a couple of parents voicing concern to a powerful little group of parents with resolve.

We decided each parent would get a letter from their doctor about how the health of their special needs child was negatively affected by the intense heat on the school bus during the summer.

The school district was approached and agreed to gather information. They were to record the temperatures in the special education buses. When it was learned that temperatures were reaching 120 degrees in the back of the bus, I wanted to cry. We had gotten their attention. The data could not be denied.

The resolution came swiftly. That summer, the school district immediately outfitted four buses with air-conditioning. They put these buses on routes with medically fragile students and promised that every bus that was retired would be replaced by one with air-conditioning. In a perfect world, we would have loved to have had all the buses outfitted with air, but we were satisfied with the compromise.

The school district probably would have eventually replaced their old buses with air-conditioned ones. Our little group just made them realize how important it was to the health of our special kids, and it happened a lot sooner.

Chapter Five

Mimi Gets Physical

You are imperfect, permanently, and inevitably flawed.
And you are beautiful.

— Amy Bloom, writer

I pulled out Mimi's baby book recently. Baby books are supposed to record the first three years of life. There are a few photos of our petite little Mimi wearing lovely frilly dresses. There she sat, with an invisible me holding her up from behind, with deep dimples and the biggest blue eyes. Those large baby blues came from the Frantz side of the family. Rick has them, and so does Katie.

Although we all wish for our children to be normal, whatever that means, it was important to me for that baby photograph to be just about Mimi. It is why the photographer helped me sit behind her, with a blanket between Mimi and me as I held her in a sitting position. No one on the planet knew how Mimi would develop from that moment forward. In the photo, she was six months old.

There were not many entries in the book when it came to milestones. They didn't happen naturally like with Katie and Ricky. Much later, instead of crawling, she combat-crawled around the house. Each of Mimi's skills was fought for as if on a messy battlefield, with countless hours of physical, occupational, and speech therapy. There were victories, to be sure, but they mostly occurred after the first three years of her life.

I had kept a record of her length, as she could not stand to measure height, up until the time she was three years old, when Mimi weighed nineteen pounds and was thirty-four inches long. As she aged, those statistics were difficult to record. Imagine weighing someone who couldn't stand on a scale. Her last recorded weight was eighty-five pounds, when Rick stood on the scale at a doctor's office by himself, and then again holding Mimi. Subtract the first number and we got eighty-five pounds! And then there was the difficulty of recording her height. Her knees were contracted from not standing or walking, and her hips were not square. Our best adult guesstimate was a little over five feet tall.

Between the pages of her baby book, I found a note from an elementary school physical therapist. At the time, Mimi was five and a half years old. The physical therapist was so proud of Mimi. Our little girl walked with a walker for a few steps, with the therapist providing maximum support at the hips. That was as far as Mimi advanced to walking on her own. She regressed to using a wheelchair sometime after that note was written.

Mimi's baby book made me a little sad. We had hoped for so much more for Mimi. We never stopped fighting for her to learn new skills — and she surprised us lots of times far beyond those early years. She was not defined by all those early milestones that did not happen. We celebrated all that she achieved!

Mimi's physical body, despite orthopedic surgeries, remained twisty. It is the only way I know to describe it. Cerebral palsy had done a disservice to her body. Her spine tilted over to one side. Her pelvis tilted forward on one side, making it appear that one leg was longer than the other. Her finger joints were loose and fragile. Mimi rolled her hands into an awkward position back toward her wrists. It was another reason to hold her hand during Mass. Her petite hands looked more normal while I was holding one of them. Thankfully, she could straighten them out. They did not stay locked into that position and did not require wrist bracing. Mimi's little toes curled under despite years of wearing AFOs (ankle foot orthotics). Her knee joints were contracted, making it impossible to straighten her legs out. That is what happens from not being able to stand or walk. Mimi's palate was small, and her teeth crowded, making it important to keep up with dental hygiene.

Personally, I tended to focus on her big blue eyes, thick black hair, toothy grin, and joyful spirit. While Mimi's twisty little body led to severe physical limitations, it didn't limit her natural, spiritual, and boundless joy.

To assist with keeping her feet and lower leg muscles and tendons stable, Mimi wore AFOs. Just for fun, we called them UFOs. Cerebral palsy was not kind to Mimi's little feet. Now, if you are going to wear shoes, your feet need to be somewhat flat on the bottom. Mimi's toes tended to curl under a little and gradually got worse over time. The solution was the AFOs. Not sure who invented them, but they are something else.

The way AFOs are made is interesting. First, the technician would cast both of Mimi's tiny feet up to just below her knees. After about twenty minutes, the cast is sliced off and they make a mold. The finished product was picked up at a much later appointment. Basically, it was hard opaque plastic with padding on the inside for the bony parts of her ankles. The plastic covered the sides and bottoms of her feet up to below her knees. They were also open a tad at the front so I could get them on her feet (with great difficulty). There were Velcro straps to hold them securely in place. I broke more than one fingernail getting them on her feet! I am certain this description is clear as mud. Trust me — they were important. After the AFOs were on her feet, I could place oversized tennis shoes over them.

So, what exactly is the purpose of such an invention? As I understood it, the theory is for the AFO to keep all those foot and ankle muscles stretched nicely so the cerebral palsy didn't mess up those feet. They also allowed us to work with her and a walker in the hope that Mimi might one day walk. The best we got was holding onto her and the walker and kind of dragging her forward. The AFOs also allowed her to stand in a stander at school so she could bear weight on her feet. Just having that sensation of standing was helpful with the alignment of her pelvis as well.

As Mimi grew, she went through several pairs of AFOs and cute little tennis shoes. With school and private physical therapy, she worked for years with a walker to no avail. She could never come close to walking independently with a walker. Mimi's hips were too unstable, and she did not have the will.

I recall an orthopedic doctor telling us one time that if a child doesn't walk by eight years old, they probably will not. I doubt that is a rule etched in Carrara marble, but it was for Mimi. And then the day came when Mimi received her first wheelchair with wheels she could independently manipulate. After that, she refused to even look at the walker. She had chosen her beloved mode of transportation, and it was enough.

The AFOs worked for many years to stabilize the muscles in her feet and ankles. Unfortunately, the padding inside them wasn't enough, and there were skin breakdowns. The muscle deformities in her ankles and feet continued to worsen and eventually forced her out of AFOs. I purchased lots of cute pairs of socks.

—

Mimi had her first orthopedic surgery when she was almost five years old. To say cerebral palsy did a number on Mimi's hips was an understatement. They were so tight that she could not sit cross-legged. Then there was her trunk, which had little stability. In fact, it never was very stable. Her back appeared very rounded. One thing you can be certain of is if you have severe enough cerebral palsy, there will be an orthopedic surgery in your future.

Mimi's first experience with orthopedic surgery included muscle releases to her hips at Texas Children's Hospital. The bone doctor was trying to do the least invasive surgery to ease those tight little hips. During surgery, he made incisions to both upper inner thighs. The idea was to make it so Mimi could open up her legs to sit up straighter. She would also be able to sit cross-legged when the muscle releases healed.

When she came out of surgery, Mimi was in a body cast. I don't recall how long she was in the hospital the first time, but they never kept us very long. Just like with most surgeries, making sure Mimi had her pain under control and was stable was all it took. In a few days, she was released to go home. The body cast was to come off in four long weeks.

Nothing prepared us for coming home though. A body cast for a small child is a curious thing. The white cast started just below her armpits and continued through her torso, with a few key interruptions, down to her pink toes, which peeked out a tad. There was a square area left open at her tummy. It was explained that children breathe with their diaphragms. That area needs to be free to move in and out. Of course, the logical spot left open is covered with a diaper. She mostly wore long baggy T-shirts. Her legs were left apart about thirty degrees, with a bar between the ankles so her hips and legs wouldn't be able to move. It was bizarre to say the least. But I was certain there was a method behind the medical madness.

Mimi was a good sport about the body cast. The whole family worked at being masters of distraction, singing songs, watching her favorite television shows, and just being silly. That was mostly Ricky's job, and he had conquered this task at the ripe age of two! Katie played the little mother. Mimi was never a complainer and adapted to her uncomfortable situation. I don't think I would have been so patient and tolerant. It looked beyond uncomfortable. The poor thing looked like a stiff stick figure.

I don't know how we made it through those four weeks. I had a calendar and marked the days off and told myself we were one step closer to the end. Mimi slept on her back each night on thick padding, with her upper body elevated. For fun, we walked her around the block, stretched out in a padded little red wagon. We "stood" her up to feed her. One of us held onto Mimi while the other spooned in her meals. Sponge baths and dry shampoo kind of helped with keeping her clean, but it was a losing battle. I could tell that cast was hot and scratchy. It couldn't come off soon enough.

Mimi's first surgery was a success. She could sit up cross-legged for the first time in her life, using her hands to prop herself up. That surgery prepared our family for the ones that were to come. We figured out creative ways to pull together as a family and get Mimi emotionally through it. It was character building for sure. After the surgery, I learned I could have been a nurse.

———

A few years later, when Mimi was seven years old, one of her hips dislocated due to the continuing effects of cerebral palsy. The same orthopedic doctor at Texas Children's Hospital recommended surgery to repair the dislocation with a plate and a pin. Rick liked the way the surgeon explained the surgery, drawing angles like an engineer would on the X-ray. The whole surgery sounded gruesome to me. The thigh bone was severed and then connected back together with a plate and pins. The goal was to achieve a certain angle with the thigh bone. Don't ask me why. The hip somehow was set back in the socket. He also would again release the muscles that were making her hips tight. The surgery was obviously more involved. I remember the surgeon telling us after the surgery how tiny her bones were. He hadn't expected to have to use tiny pediatric pins during the surgery.

This time, Mimi was to stay in the body cast for six weeks. Due to the severed thigh bone needing to heal, it was several weeks before we could stand her upright with the cast on. Not only was six weeks a long time, but the cast didn't seem to be padded well at the lower back. When I noticed blood at the back of the cast after a diaper change, I panicked. Mimi came out of the cast one week early. Her tailbone protruded, and the cast was not adequately padded for all the pressure.

I remember holding Mimi's hand as the huge and cumbersome body cast was noisily sawed off. I sang songs to distract Mimi from crying. It only helped a little. Although it didn't hurt, it was so very noisy and seemed to take forever. They sawed it off in two pieces as if it were a clam shell. There was the top of the cast and the bottom. I was so relieved to be done with it. Mimi was older, bigger, and it was all just so much more difficult.

I will never forget the moment the cast was cut completely away. The top half of the cast was carefully removed. However, when we tried to lift Mimi out of the bottom of the cast, she screamed. It was finally determined the cast had become her comfort zone. She was not ready to give it up. After the orthopedic doctor treated the bloody tailbone area, he recommended putting her back in the cast for a few days. The two halves were put back together around Mimi, with lots of extra padding at the tailbone. Instead of recasting, Ace bandages were wound around the cast so Mimi would feel secure. That night she slept in her cocoon cast. It was a few days before we were able to ease her out of the cast.

It was many years later at an annual orthopedic X-ray appointment that Rick and I were given the news the same hip had again dislocated. Cerebral palsy continued to move her little bones and tighten her muscles like a stiff rubber band. She had also developed a pelvic obliquity. That means her pelvis was not square, which made it seem like one leg was shorter than the other. Since it was not giving Mimi any pain, the surgeon did not recommend further surgery.

—

Mimi was a young teenager when the next set of three orthopedic surgeries was performed. Mimi could no longer wear the AFOs that kept the muscles in her feet stretched. This meant her toes slowly drew up, and her feet distorted. Mimi could no longer wear shoes. Instead, Mimi wore cute little socks.

During the winter, it was difficult to keep those little feet warm. My mother and I knitted custom leg warmers. My mother also knitted thick slippers to place over her socks. Still, Rick and I thought maybe we should visit an orthopedic doctor and see if there was a surgery that would allow her to wear shoes. Mimi also had circulation issues, which kept her feet cold to the touch.

I don't recall who gave us the recommendation. We took Mimi to a pediatric orthopedic surgeon near the medical center. His solution was a surgery with external rods and pins and a metal cage over her lower leg down to the bottom of her foot. We opted to have the most distorted foot operated on first. This foot also had lots of swelling at the top. It was explained there would be a series of three surgeries on the first foot over a six-month period.

The first surgery involved placing the external fixation rods, pins, and the outer cage (they called it a "halo," which seemed appropriate). The multiple metal rods went through her lower leg. The spots where the long pins exited her skin were covered with little spongy pads. I was responsible for changing out the pads daily. Not only that. There were a couple of spots where a wrench was applied to screws that were attached to the rods, and the screws turned slowly each day. This accomplished moving the bones slowly.

The hospital stay lasted a few interesting days. I recall that late on the first day one of the nurses was trying to figure out Mimi's pain level. She held a poster made of smiley and frowny faces. I tried to explain to the nurse that Mimi was doing fine. I hadn't left her side, and the pain medication in her

IV was working like a champ. But the nurse persisted in engaging Mimi and ignoring me. She insisted Mimi point to the smiley face that corresponded to her level of pain. Mimi did not look like the happy faces on the poster. I then asked the nurse to step away from in front of the television. It turned out that Mimi was fine — it was just that she had been immersed in a *SpongeBob SquarePants* marathon prior to the nurse's arrival, and she was quite grumpy about not being able to watch it. The nurse exited Mimi's room, taking the smiley face poster with her.

Caring for Mimi during these months was again a family project. Katie and Ricky kept her distracted. Bathing was difficult, because none of the wound openings could be immersed in water. My engineer husband had an interesting solution. By the time of the surgery, we had renovated one of our bathrooms to become a large handicapped bathroom, so Rick and Ricky blew up a child's wading pool right in the bathroom and filled it partway with water. We took Mimi's bath chair and placed it in the pool instead of the bathtub. Her affected leg was propped up and slung over the edge of the wading pool. Katie and I took over after the boys left the bathroom. We poured water over her hair and body and soaped and rinsed to get her nice and clean. After we were finished and Mimi was dressed, the boys lifted her out of the pool and emptied it.

Sleeping was another challenge. Mimi had to sleep on her back on thick foam that we covered with a sheet, with her head propped higher than her feet. I don't know how she slept for six months in that condition.

The next surgery was to fuse her ankle so it would not move and distort. The surgeon also performed an additional surgery to remove bone from the back of her hip at the same time. He used her own bone to fuse her ankle. Since Mimi wasn't ever going to walk, the goal was for her foot and ankle to not distort.

The final surgery was to take the pins, rods, and external fixations off. This was my favorite surgery, as it was all going to be over. It was also the most difficult emotionally, because when we accompanied Mimi to the holding area, she got this horrible look on her face. She must have suddenly remembered where she was and didn't want to go. It was the only time Mimi loudly complained. Rick and I cried buckets that she would have to go through yet another surgery.

After all the metal was finally taken off her leg, she was put in a cast from below the knee down to her foot a couple of times. One cast was baby blue, and the next was hot pink. We weren't told there was going to be casting involved. Why this was left out of the doctor's conversation with the patient's family, I'll never know.

We didn't broadcast the surgery to anyone outside our little circle. I don't know why we were so private about the whole thing. Certainly, 99 percent of the people at church didn't know. We simply placed a small blanket over her legs to cover up the wire cage when she attended Mass. Later, when the cage came off and the cast appeared, we continued with the small blanket routine.

—

In 2001, I wrote a column in *The Observer* newspaper about one of the three hospital stays. It was the most controversial humor column I ever wrote. I received my only "hate" mail in the form of a letter to the editor of *The Observer*. I was devastated and cried a whole box of Kleenex over it. To think a person spent the time to write and mail a nasty letter with no return address about a humor column, so it could be published for lots of people to read. I just didn't understand. It wasn't like now, when so many people spew poisonous venom so freely on social media. For some reason, the person just didn't think it appropriate to write about staying overnight in a hospital with our daughter. I'll let you be the judge.

The Observer
You Gotta Laugh — "Hospital Stay Tests Survival Skills"
Written by Dixie Frantz
Published January 24, 2001

Feelin' a bit like a veteran survivor these days after successfully completing two hospital stays in the past month with our young daughter. Our adventure into shark infested- waters reminds me of the recent "Cast Away" movie with all-around good guy Tom Hanks. Yep, simulated crashing in an airplane, being deserted on a remote island, snoozing on rocks, and eating yucky stuff. Our most recent captivity lasted several very long days until finally being rescued. By the way, loved the movie, but the ending ... come on. What was that all about?

Yeah, hubby and I thought we were prepared for an uneventful plane ride, so to speak, by the capable surgeon. But when it finally came down to leaving the holding area and saying goodbye to our little girl before surgery, the churning stomachs took over. Just imagine two parents holding onto a pitching life raft for five hours in the surgery waiting room. That was definitely us. Then suddenly, the waters calm with the simple utterance of three small words by the physician: "She's just fine." Yippee, the surviving parents had finally made it to shore.

So, we finally sail Mimi up to her room after recovery. The place reminded me of the barren tropical island before Tom Hanks took up residence. The bare essentials for survival were all there, but it took a couple of hours of poking around before we got our compass bearings. Let's just say hospital beds have changed immensely since our last hospital stay ten years before. Did ya know they have the "bother the nurse" buttons, "make the bed go up and down" keypad, and the "flood the room with very bright lights" switch all carefully hidden on flat little pads in the bed's guardrails? Now just when did they get rid of the large obvious remote thingy?

Think the first night in the hospital was probably the worst as far as getting any sleep goes. And I'm not just referring to the multiple checking of vital signs like temperature and corpuscle pressure in the middle of the p.m. Of course, I jumped up and down with delight at the sight of the skimpy chair that folded out into a facsimile of a bumpy bed. In the olden days, moms and/or dads slept sitting at ninety degrees in rickety chairs all night. In some hospitals, I suppose it's likely still the case.

The whole sleeping thing started off rather badly when I made the mistake of snoozing in my street clothes in the sub-zero meat locker environment. And did I mention snuggling up under only ONE of the hospital's excessively linty and paper-thin white blankets? Don't ask me what I was thinkin', because obviously I wasn't. Too much tropical sun, I guess. As if the ice cubes in my socks weren't sad enough, you should have seen the condition of my wrinkly attire the next morning. And my black britches, being slightly fuzzy in nature, were entirely covered in stubborn white lint. I'm taking bets there is a certain sadistic someone adding a couple cups of lint balls and Elmer's glue, along with the detergent in the hospital laundry room. It's why I switched the next night to wearing pj's and covering up with three lovely lint-encrusted hospital blankies. Oh yeah, the name of game is called "learn from your mistakes" and I play it so well.

And did I tell you that we had our own "Wilson" at the hospital? In the "Cast Away" flick, Tom Hanks befriends a volleyball that floats up on the beach in a Federal Express box. We called our friend Nerf. Actually, he's a small, squishy soccer ball Mimi and her dad tossed around the hospital room when daytime television got to be a tad too much. And just like Wilson, it was a sad day when Nerf mysteriously disappeared. I suspect one of the nurses made off with our friend after she accidentally got beaned on the head the second day of our confinement.

But it was partaking of the yucky food that was probably the worst part of being stuck in the hospital. Each day I'd circle logical choices from a menu that had strange phrases printed on it for a hospital menu ... foreign sounding jargon like "sumptuously prepared to perfection" and "delicately seasoned." Who were they trying to snowball? Nothin' that Mimi received on a tray from the kitchen remotely resembled "sumptuous."

For the sake of future patients, I made a couple of hopefully helpful culinary suggestions to the exit questionnaire regarding our hospital visit. Thought there should be a couple of added menu selections with callout phone numbers from local eatery establishments for Chinese food and pizza at the very least. Obviously, the small hospital we were marooned on did not have a Mickey D's.

We were finally rescued on day four of our confinement. Mimi had just tugged her IV out again, so they decided to send us packing one night earlier than expected. Hospitals ... a tolerable place to visit, but I wouldn't want to be marooned there for longer than a few days.

The following week, the newspaper printed a bunch of positive letters from readers in opposition to the hate letter. It was a teachable moment for me. I wasn't ever going to give up or change the way I wrote my columns — and the thick skin that was generated as a result of the experience made me invincible.

—

We were glad that we tried to get Mimi into shoes. It could have worked. But ultimately, there was no way we were going to put her through three surgeries on the other foot. The climb up and down that mountain several times wasn't worth the view. Ultimately, the operated foot drew up and it became impossible for her to wear a shoe on it.

—

As if orthopedic issues weren't challenging enough, there were always the not-so-fun trips to the dentist that were a huge challenge for Mimi — and for me.

Now, children need regular dental visits. That is a given. So do children with special needs. Did you know children with special needs often have issues like mouth breathing and medications that negatively affect their teeth? Some children fall due to seizures and harm their teeth, and others just have difficulty with dental hygiene.

Mimi never learned to brush her teeth. It was something they worked on in school. It remained on her IEP for many years. If you handed Mimi a toothbrush, she knew what to do with it. If she managed to hit one of her teeth with the toothbrush, it was a victory. It was just not something she ever mastered. I brushed her teeth in the morning and before bed, only wetting the toothbrush. One reason was because she couldn't spit out the water. The other was because the one time I used toothpaste, she immediately threw up. Thankfully, she never had any cavities.

Of course, you actually have to have teeth to have them cleaned. Mimi's teeth did not even emerge until she was about three years old.

Through a great recommendation, I found a local pediatric dentist. It turned out he had done his residency at a state school, or a state institution. He assured me Mimi was not his most difficult dental patient. He had several patients with special needs.

For many years, he took care of Mimi and did a great job. But the dental appointment was never the easiest to get through. In fact, it was my least favorite thing to do on the planet. I still shiver when I think about it. I learned through friends that by its very nature, going to the dentist is traumatic for lots of children with special needs. I could see why a parent might stop taking their special child to the dentist. But they are often the very population that needs to go the most.

From a child's perspective, imagine a horror movie where a bad guy holds you down and comes at you with a metal utensil trying to rip your throat out. Not at all the case, but I always felt certain Mimi might have felt that way.

I only made my biggest dentist-related mistake one time. Mimi had an appointment mid-morning after breakfast. A few minutes into the exam and teeth cleaning, Mimi's breakfast came up all over the dentist, Mimi, me, and the assistant helping me hold her down. That was the fastest teeth cleaning ever — and no X-rays.

After that traumatic fiasco, I always made sure Mimi was the dentist's first appointment, and there was no breakfast until after the cleaning. I knew what that bad gag reflex could do and wanted the dental office to keep inviting us back! Before starting the exam and cleaning, the dentist always asked if Mimi had eaten first. We both chuckled about it. Obviously, he was going to ask.

Next, the not-so-fun part started. An assistant and I held Mimi down the best we could while the dentist worked his magic. Mimi was little but strong, and boy could she squirm. She didn't like anyone working in her mouth. The sweat poured through my shirt as I did my part. It amazed me how after each teeth cleaning Mimi was so willing to give the dentist a hug. She never held it against him and lifted her long arms up for a hug after the foaming fluoride was applied to her sparkling teeth. Me, on the other hand, if I was a drinkin' girl, I would have headed straight to the bar for a margarita on the rocks, no salt, at ten a.m.

The ride home was quiet on my part as I calmed myself down. Mimi held her new toothbrush in her left hand and happily said the word "teeth."

Certainly, Mimi lived in the moment. She had no worries or anxieties about the future or what happened next. I was not certain if she was proud of her smile or glad it was over. Once home, I fed her a hearty breakfast of pancakes and watched for a spell to make sure her breakfast stayed where it belonged.

—

Many years down the road, we found a dentist who offered IV sedation for his patients with special needs. Thank you to my friend Mary for the recommendation! This procedure does not come cheap. Back a few years ago, it was about one thousand dollars for a teeth cleaning, X-rays, and sedation.

I had several friends who swore by the procedure for their adults with special needs. The dental office was about an hour away. I remember the first time Rick and I took Mimi for the sedation appointment. We watched as the anesthesiologist inserted the IV in her hand, which wasn't easy, and dripped the sedation medication. Mimi was very cooperative with this part of the appointment, and in just a few seconds she was fast asleep. I didn't really like the whole idea of having to sedate her for a routine cleaning, but this was so much less traumatic than the way we had always had her teeth cleaned in the past. We also knew if the dentist found a tooth that needed work, he could take care of it while she was sedated.

—

Speaking of important members of Mimi's care team — a great pediatrician made all the difference. I am not sure what led me to Dr. Penn. I feel certain someone gave me a stellar recommendation. But I believe there was a little divine intervention with lots of glitter sprinkled in. He was one pediatrician in a group of about five or six other pediatricians. Over the years, he provided exceptional care for both Katie and Mimi, and later for Ricky. From the beginning, Dr. Penn really listened to my concerns, and together we brainstormed real solutions. I valued his opinion. He assisted in so many areas over the long years of Mimi's care. He was a valued and trusted member of our team.

One interesting part of Dr. Penn's practice is his love of magic. After an office visit, if there was time, he would perform a magic trick to delight his patients and their parents. For the little ones, he might bring in a puppet and perform. For Mimi, it was always all about the puppets. I could see how these little things formed a bond between doctor and patient, and I admired him for his knowledge as a physician and his whimsy.

Years later, when Ricky was born, Dr. Penn always tried to bring in a new magic trick to entertain Ricky. The little dude loved it! I recall riding in the car after an office visit, with Ricky going on and on in the back seat trying to figure out just how Dr. Penn had performed a trick.

When Mimi left Dr. Penn's care, it was a sad day. I mean, it had to end someday. What was I going to do without him?

Several years later, Dr. Penn called me. At his suggestion, Mimi and I met Dr. Penn for lunch several times at a local deli on a Saturday. One time he brought his lovely wife. I think Mimi held his hand for most of the first lunch. She adored him as much as I did.

After Mimi's death, Dr. Penn came to Mimi's visitation. What a sad look he had on his face that day. I know his expression mirrored my own.

—

There have been a couple of sweet young ladies I let into our inner sanctum who helped our family so much. A big challenge at our house after Ricky and Katie left the nest was bathing Mimi. Bathing a wheel-chair-bound adult with little trunk support is a huge challenge.

When Mimi was little and didn't weigh much more than a feather, I lifted her into the bathtub onto an infant bath sponge. Just a few inches of water in the tub was all I needed as I poured warm water onto her soapy body. Easy peasy! I did it by myself for years. As Mimi grew, this wasn't possible. We eventually purchased a bath chair made with a frame of PVC pipe and covered with blue mesh. The chair had the ability to lean back like a beach chair, so there were no worries about difficulties because of Mimi's lack of trunk stability. I poured water from a plastic cup onto her long hair and washed it first before moving down to her body. When Katie was home, she helped me with the two-person lift out of the tub onto a thick towel. For many years, Ricky and Mimi's dad also assisted after Mimi was covered with a towel.

After our family nest emptied out, Rick and I bathed Mimi with modesty protocols put in place by me. After a few years, I decided a little help would lighten the load for Rick. The weekday evenings were so short when Mimi had to be bathed. When I met Heather, I knew I had found someone with a huge heart who could make our evenings less stressful. Very often Heather would come over before Rick got home from work. Now, if you had stood outside the bathroom door and listened, you would have thought there was a party in there. Along with her loving heart, Heather had a beautiful singing voice, and Mimi loved her.

After Heather went off to medical school, I approached Jessica, who worked at the day center Mimi attended. Another young lady with a loving, giving heart, she helped me bathe Mimi for several months before cancer reared its ugly head at our house.

In 2014, I wrote a column for *The Tribune* about the lovely Heather, a shining example of the many people in our lives who made a difficult task an adventure.

The Tribune
You Gotta Laugh — "Ode to Heather"
Written by Dixie Frantz
Published July 14, 2014

Our special needs daughter turned thirty big ones the other day. I'm still trying to wrap my exploding head around that one. It is probably why I am sitting here reflecting ... and thinking about the amazing "journey" our family has traveled so far with Mimi. While the yellow brick road hasn't always been so smooth ... tripped a couple of times over some loose bricks ... and a couple of overgrown tree roots ... I can safely say we still have our ruby red slippers with sparkly sequins intact. Wicked witches and flying monkeys beware. We carry multiple indestructible magic wands in our back pockets.

Over the years, I have been a witness to many amazing people that continue to pass through Mimi's interesting life as we skip toward Oz. All those cheerful bus drivers delivering Mimi and her wheelchair home in the pouring rain comes to mind. There have also been dedicated teachers, amazing therapists, skilled orthopedic surgeons, sleepless summer camp buddies, lovely classroom aides ... oh and I'm just getting started.

Some have shown to have the gray matter of a most intellectual scarecrow ... like Miss Marie. Only she is way cuter than Ray Bolger with hay hangin' out of his sleeves! It takes lots of imagination for a therapist to teach a skill a hundred different ways like, for instance, a pincer grasp. Babies between nine and 12 months of age usually learn that little milestone of using their thumb and index finger together to perform a task. I think Mimi was in middle school when it was finally checked off! And a most ginormous check mark it was! Covered one whole wall and the ceiling in our family room.

Did I mention I ran into Marie the other day at the beauty parlor? We were both getting the color of our roots altered. Marie was Mimi's occupational therapist all those years ago. I still tease her about teaching Mimi to pinch people. I say that with a Cheshire cat grin across my thankful face. Just try and pick up a slippery blue M&M without using those two fingers. I dare you!

I have also been an eyewitness to a bunch of people with the heart of the Tin Man with the way they cared for Mimi. Makes me think of the days when we visited our pediatrician. Dr. Penn, our local physician/magician, was a great doctor for all my kids, but especially Mimi. Then despite my best plans ... the kids grew up. Don't you hate when that happens?

Every couple of years, Dr. Penn emails to set up a lunch date with Mimi. Who does that? We meet at a local deli, Mimi hugs Dr. Penn a hundred times like it was yesterday and we chat about how glorious life is.

I saved Heather for last! Last year I was looking to hire someone to help me bathe Mimi. I met Heather at her mother's doctor's office while Mimi was having her yearly physical. We got to chatting. Heather mentioned she would be hanging out for a year until she started medical school. One thing led to another and pretty soon Heather was the one who made bath time a party at our house. For 11 months, there was lots of singing, hugging and new hairdos on Mimi.

Heather recently left us for medical school. I wish her the very best! Her visits will always be fondly remembered ... just like watching reruns of the happiest parts of "The Wizard of Oz."

Chapter Six
The Spirit Moves Her

Scatter joy.

– Ralph Waldo Emerson

Mimi was a very spiritual little being. If you looked deep into her eyes, you might have seen that spark. You might not have been able to explain it, but you knew there was something different about Mimi that had nothing to do with cerebral palsy. I believe most of her young spiritual life was developed due to the influences of her church, parents, older sister, and little brother, who all made a lasting impact by living their faith. But it all started with a spiritual spark.

I taught religious education for a couple of years with Mimi in my class. Back then I taught in our home once a week during the school year. I felt comfortable including Mimi, Ricky, and a handful of other young children. The lessons were simple. I felt it was possible Mimi could understand the love of our faith at that level.

As Mimi got a little older, classes were on church grounds. I volunteered to be an aide and assisted the teacher in Mimi's class. Stepping back from some of the teacher responsibilities, I was able to make sure there were not any issues with Mimi being in the class. I did not want to take anything for granted.

Eventually, Mimi moved to a classroom where I was not involved in teaching or as an aide. I stepped back to see what happened. The teacher was supportive and so were the children. I learned to hover less as the years flew by, but there were religious hurdles yet to be jumped over.

—

Rick and I agonized over whether Mimi should receive Holy Communion for the first time. We talked about it often after she reached the age of seven, when most receive the sacrament. Since her speech was so limited, it was impossible for us to know if she understood the magnitude of the sacrament.

Mimi had participated formally in Catholic education during her elementary school years, but still we couldn't make up our minds if it was appropriate. Several times one of us talked to Father Tinney, founding pastor at our church, St. Martha Catholic Church. Father clearly advised us that he was fine with Mimi receiving Holy Communion. Still, we hesitated.

Fast-forward three years and it was time for Ricky to receive his first Holy Communion. He was easy. But the topic was brought up in our house again about Mimi. By then, we had a new pastor, Father Brinkman. I made an appointment and restarted the conversation. I told him we could not be sure she fully understood the concept of Holy Communion. I mean ... how could we know? Mimi spoke barely a hundred words at that time. I told him how we had talked several times to Father Tinney a few years back about our dilemma. Rick had even discussed it with several priest friends. Father Brinkman told me that certainly Mimi should receive Holy Communion. He said there was no reason in his mind to exclude her from the sacrament. The only thing stopping her was confession, and he expected me to make that happen.

When I reported back to Rick that Father Brinkman told me Mimi would indeed be receiving her first Holy Communion, Rick caved. Now all I had to do was take Mimi to confession. As Hamlet would say, "Therein lies the rub." What exactly was Mimi going to confess?

I know what you are thinking. What happened next? Well, I thought a lot about that. I knew if I wheeled Mimi into the confessional, turned around, and closed the door on the two of them, Mimi would say "hi" really loud and throw up her arms for a hug. I didn't want to put Father Brinkman in that position. Nope! That would NOT be the recipe for an official confession in my book. So instead, I wheeled Mimi into the confessional and sat myself down next to her.

I started with, "Bless her, Father, for Mimi has sinned. This is her first confession."

Then I told him how I had personally witnessed Mimi intentionally pulling her brother's hair several times. That was it. Pure and simple, that was the only thing I had personally witnessed Mimi ever doing that could be remotely construed as "sinful." Ricky and Mimi's relationship was complicated and funny. I truly think she did it to get his attention and pull rank. After all, Mimi was the older sister.

"That's all I got, Father," I said.

He promptly let me know that Mimi would not be forgiven for pulling her brother's hair. He did not believe Mimi was capable of sinning and so he did not believe she needed to be forgiven. All that preparing and sweating and squeezing Mimi and her wheelchair into the confessional was for naught. He did not have to tell me I was living with a saint. I intuitively felt it, but didn't want to project it on Father Brinkman. So, I thanked Father for listening to Mimi's attempt at confession. Then, I slowly turned Mimi and her wheelchair around in the small confessional and left. That was the last time Mimi went to confession. She never did anything worse than pull her brother's hair. Sometimes a mother needs to just shut up and trust a pastor's advice. He is, after all, the spiritual expert.

Over the decades, there have been several traditions for children to celebrate their first Holy Communion at St. Martha. Katie received her first Holy Communion at a special Mass on a Saturday afternoon. Individual children occasionally would celebrate with their family at Mass. That is what we did for Mimi and Ricky.

We opted to have it during the eleven o'clock Mass. It was the Mass our family attended almost exclusively. It was comfortable. People knew us. Rick had his brother, Gary, take photographs of our big family event. We just sat in our family's usual spot in the front row by the choir, where there was a short bench next to which we could park Mimi's wheelchair. The old church didn't have handicapped seating near the front, but this short row had always been our perfect spot.

When it was time for Holy Communion, the priest, Father Romanus, came over to our pew. Rick and Father Romanus had this special relationship, and we loved that he was able to share this special moment. Rick served with Father Romanus once a week during Thursday's early 6:30 a.m. daily Mass in the chapel. This task was usually performed by a trained teenager, but that early in the morning, they were still in bed. The crowd was mostly people heading to work after Mass. Rick had been an altar server when he was young and was totally at ease with altar serving duties.

When the moment finally arrived for Communion, Rick stood on one side of Mimi. I stood on the other. I didn't realize how very long the actual moments of Mimi receiving Holy Communion were until I saw the photos. There were six or seven progressive photos of Rick and I standing on each side of Mimi getting ready to help with the host. There was one of Mimi not opening her mouth and several others of the host approaching her open mouth. Finally, the host (actually half of a host, since her mouth was so small) connects with her tongue. But that is not all. Rick and I both stand still waiting for her to swallow the host for a couple of photos. While all this was going on, Father Romanus had moved on to give Ricky and Katie Communion. There was a deodorant fail on my part that day.

Holy Communion after that was never easy. I always assisted with making sure the host made it into Mimi's mouth and stayed there. Some eucharistic ministers passed her by and Rick and I had to signal one over to Mimi. The best possible scenario was for Mimi to be given part of a host rather than a whole one. She has a small mouth, and the gag reflex was always an issue to be considered. Sometimes the priest or eucharistic minister wasn't paying any attention to my signal and charged forward with a whole host. Mimi never choked — thank you, Jesus. Divine intervention for sure!

—

For most of her life, Mimi attended Mass with her family each Sunday. Two exceptions would be when Mimi was recovering from an orthopedic surgery, and for most of 2016, when Rick was battling an illness.

We never told anyone Mimi had cerebral palsy. Not in the beginning. I mean, how do you even bring up the subject? I didn't. One of the first clues that Mimi was different were her eyes. They would cross slightly. Not all the time. I noticed it more when she was tired. It is called strabismus. Thank goodness her eyesight was remarkable. Mimi never needed glasses, and there was no need to subject her to eye surgery.

When Mimi was little, until about five years old, I carried her into Mass on my hip. She was so petite, with thin arms and legs, weighing twenty pounds at three years old. She sat on my lap. Like most parents with little children, we sat in the back of the church. Ricky was three years younger, and with two little ones, the back of the church was a bit of a safe haven. Also, Mimi was sensitive to babies crying and couldn't stop herself from crying in sympathy. She had a very tender heart and just couldn't stand to hear other babies cry. It was so difficult for her to get her emotions back under control that she would often have to be taken out of the church for a time. Once her crying — more like sobbing — started, there was no stopping her for several minutes. There was no way to explain this to people.

As Mimi aged, I could use the art of distraction by taking out my wallet and showing Mimi photographs. Certain songs like "Silent Night" caused Mimi to sob. It is a beautiful song, but to Mimi I suspected it sounded very sad. If I couldn't get my wallet out in time, I resorted to whispering what would happen after Mass — maybe going out to lunch.

It was a given that Mimi couldn't be carried into church forever. Her thin legs grew longer. She was easy to lift but awkward to carry around. The first time I wheeled her into Mass, I could feel the heat rise in my face. Her first wheelchair was more like a large stroller, but it screamed wheelchair. I didn't want anyone to see her any differently than as the little girl I carried on my hip in frilly dresses, with matching bright bows in her long, dark hair. It was so painful the first time. Maybe people had looked at our little Mimi all along and wondered what was different. They might not have been able to put their finger on it. Now they would look at Mimi and think about her in a different way.

From that day on, I held one of her hands during Mass. It felt right to both of us. If one of us let go, the other would seek the other's hand. It was comforting and it made us feel deeply and spiritually connected in those moments at Mass. It also helped with not letting Mimi grab someone passing by for Holy Communion to garner a hug.

In the old church, there was no accessible seating in the front to accommodate wheelchairs. This was a challenge. From the back, Mimi couldn't see anything happening on the altar. We located a short pew near the choir. We had found our front row and claimed it until the new church was built.

When the new church campus was finished, there was handicapped seating in a few of the front pews. We tried to claim our spot, making sure to get to Mass early. Mimi seemed to pay close attention to what was happening on the altar. When the "Our Father" was recited, Mimi would lean over and whisper "Sonic." She knew Mass was nearly over and the possibility we would stop for a to-go lunch might be in her future.

The only other exception to Mimi attending Mass was the year Rick was diagnosed with stage 4 kidney cancer. It was early 2016. Rick was so sick he couldn't physically help me lift Mimi out of her wheelchair to attend Mass in the family car. Instead, a eucharistic minister came to our house and gave Mimi Holy Communion. It took two people to lift Mimi into the back seat of my car and then take apart her wheelchair and stow it in the back.

We now saw the necessity for a wheelchair-accessible vehicle and started working on what that car would look like for Mimi. It needed to be a family car that I could get Mimi into easily without taking her out of her wheelchair. We knew there was a state program that helped with funding part of the modification for a new vehicle. We had to figure out what type of vehicle we needed, where to purchase it, and then how to access the state program. We knew it would not be like heading down to the local dealership and driving off the lot the next day with the perfect car. This was going to be a project.

All those years of attending Mass with Mimi deeply influenced people. Before and after Mass, Mimi found lots of opportunities to hug parishioners. Sometimes there would even be a line. Mimi savored those moments. It was my job to try to unlock her hands from someone's neck. Sometimes I apologized and offered to pay for a chiropractic adjustment. Thankfully, no one took me up on the offer. Hugging was a huge part of who Mimi was.

Taking Mimi into Mass in that first wheelchair was the most difficult. I got over it and moved on. I also learned Mimi did not hum during Mass.

Humming was a repetitive pastime of hers that sounded like one very long note. If she had, we might have camped out in the cry room (a room designated for families with crying babies and their families), our whole lives. That would have impeded her ability to share her hugging ministry. Again, divine intervention!

I wrote a column in 2007 for *The Tribune* about hugs in church and about a nice man named Mr. Buddy's accidental run-in with Mimi.

The Tribune
You Gotta Laugh — "The Hug Doctor Is In"
Written by Dixie Frantz
Published September 12, 2007

I was doing a little research for this week's "hug" column and came across some interesting snippets. Did you know that next year will mark the twenty-fifth anniversary of National Hug Week? When you purchase your 2008 calendar in a couple of months, be sure and highlight in yellow marker May 4 through 10, so you don't miss out on the celebration.

Oh, and you may have heard about the official "hug prescription," but it certainly bears, as in great big bear hugs, repeating. The Hugs for Health Foundation home page lists a daily prescription, which the Frantz household has practiced for centuries. Administer four hugs daily for survival, eight for maintenance, and twelve for growth. The Frantz family lands somewhere in the "hug" realm of way past growth into ludicrous.

We prefer to lavish credit on Mimi, our special needs daughter, who is known far and wide for her extraordinary hugs, and for catapulting the Frantz family on the path to extreme hug fitness. Heck, Mimi has for years handed them out to most anyone who gets close enough. One of our major challenges is she doesn't like to let go. I'm considering asking Dr. Charlie, our local chiropractor extraordinaire, if he has any five dollars off coupons for major spine realignments. I could carry them in my purse and dole out to those who encounter a potential debilitating "Mimi" head lock.

Of course, the girl has certainly gotten herself in a dill pickle on occasion. It was in her first year of middle school that hugging was suddenly deemed not so appropriate. Mimi's special education teachers had their hands full trying to convince the lass about the value of shaking hands instead of reaching out for a nearby neck to wrap her arms around. I believe greeting another appropriately with a handshake was listed as one of her goals and objectives from the beginning of middle school through most of high school. While we tried to support the school with positive reinforcement at home, the Frantz family never minded much that Mimi flunked hand shaking. In the grand scheme of things, hugging pretty much defines her as a person.

Now wouldn't you know it, last week at church, Mimi had her first "hug" casualty. Mr. Buddy ran over to Mimi after Mass for his big embrace. His lovely wife, Pat, was close behind and lamented that Buddy had beat her to the punch. As I stood behind Mimi's wheelchair, Buddy carefully leaned over as Mimi wrapped her long thin arms firmly around his neck and affectionately squeezed and squealed in his right ear. They hadn't seen each for a spell, so it was an extra-long hug. It wasn't until we arrived home after church that I learned Buddy had a run-in with Mimi's wheelchair.

"Did you know that Buddy received a nasty scratch from Mimi's wheelchair?" hubby indicated.

Rick had ushered that Sunday and happened to be standing in the back when Buddy passed by a few minutes after the big hug-fest. Horrified when I heard the news, I stood in the kitchen imagining our friend being carried out the back of the church on a stretcher with a tourniquet on one arm, and it was all Mimi's fault.

"You should have seen Pat emptying out her purse in the pew with all sorts of first aid supplies. I swear she must have been a girl scout when she was little," Rick laughed.

"Or perhaps she is so well prepared because she is a grandma," I added.

A few days later Buddy received a get-well card from Mimi which also contained a Sponge Bob Square Pants band aid for his boo-boo. I know the card assisted in his speedy recovery because of the lovely e-mail I received a few days later from Pat. It read: "The card and the band aid were just too cute. Buddy is just fine. It tickled him to death to hear from Mimi. We love her so much. Tell Mimi the band aid did the trick. He is healed. LOL, Pat and Buddy"

So, if you happen across the Frantz family in your daily travels, don't be bashful. Dr. Mimi is always available to fill your hug prescription. Just be mindful of the wheelchair.

—

Back when our kids were little, we used to attend the children's Mass on Christmas Eve, which featured a Christmas pageant. There is something so inspiring about seeing young children recreate the very first Christmas.

For several years, I thought it would be wonderful to have Mimi in the pageant. But she was getting older and close to the age cutoff. If this was going to happen, it had to be the year she was nine or ten.

Finally, I worked up the nerve to go to the planning meeting. Oh, and I talked Ricky into also participating. At first, he wasn't too keen on my idea. However, I can be persuasive. I knew what made Ricky tick. My easygoing son was eager to please, especially when I called it an "adventure."

I don't recall how it was determined what role the children received, but I was happy that Mimi would be one of the many angels. It was a perfect fit. Ricky would be a scruffy shepherd. Both of our children had certainly been given the correct roles.

I made the two costumes. Nothing too complicated. Mimi's was made from a white sheet and it was much easier than some of the Halloween costumes I had previously stitched on the old Singer sewing machine. Rick and Katie helped with Mimi's glittery yellow cardboard angel wings, which we affixed to the back of her wheelchair frame. With Katie's craft experience and Rick's engineering prowess, we couldn't go wrong. My only issue was that Ricky had to wear a wrap on his head. I doubted it would stay on for long, but reasoned that if he made it down the aisle with the headgear on his head, it would be a huge win!

A few weeks before the big event, there were several evening practices in the church. Mimi and Ricky had to saunter down the aisle and turn around to face the parish. One of the older "angels" would push Mimi, turn, and engage one of her wheelchair brakes so she couldn't wander. I worried more about Ricky, since he tended to fidget. Thankfully, it was the little children portraying the holy family who had the most challenging parts.

When Christmas Eve finally approached, I wondered if it was all a huge mistake. What was I trying to prove by having Mimi in the pageant? Would people take her inclusion the wrong way? There was no way to ask Mimi if she even wanted to participate, or to get a proper answer. I had this last-minute struggle with myself and finally reasoned that there was so little opportunity for Mimi to participate in such things in life. Why not? At the very least, she could be an angel in a Christmas pageant.

Both Mimi and Ricky looked adorable in their costumes. Ricky even kept his head wrap on his head until the photographs were taken after Mass. He fidgeted a little, but so did some of the other shepherds. Mimi performed her role perfectly, sitting there quietly with the other angels. I was so proud of all the children that night.

The following year when the Christmas pageant neared, a few mothers asked me if Mimi was going to participate again. They had enjoyed her being in the pageant. It made me smile that they even remembered. I let them know it was one of those once-in-a-lifetime kind of things. But to my way of thinking, the Christmas pageant confirmed it. Mimi was an angel.

In 1999, I wrote a column in *The Observer* about Mimi and Ricky's participation in the Christmas pageant at our church.

The Observer
You Gotta Laugh — "Christmas Pageants and Angels"
Written by Dixie Frantz
Published December 22, 1999

"Does anyone have thoughts about which Christmas Mass we should attend this year?" I queried the week before Christmas with all assembled at the dinner table. There are about seven choices and each one has their own unique personality. The lively debate continued for the next several days.

When our kids were little, we always attended the Children's Mass on Christmas Eve. Every year for the entire month of December, Father would warn his flock that it was the rowdiest. Anyone expecting a solemn celebration better plan on attending another Mass. It's a certainty he was referring to the annual Nativity Pageant put on with little children posing as Mary and Joseph. Supporting cast included wiggly shepherds, cutesy little lasses decked out in angel garb, and the three semi-wise boys. And did I forget to mention the very patient mothers who organized the cantankerous crew? I'm certain there's a special place in Heaven with aisles of bathtubs filled with perpetual foaming bubbles and crates of imported chocolates for past directors of the annual Christmas pageants at our church.

It was about eight or maybe nine years ago, when I decided that Ricky and Mimi had to have that "pageant experience" to add to their childhood list of memories. It entered my mind that they would probably nail me on it someday from a psychiatrist's couch. I can hear Ricky now.

"It was my mother who forced me to participate in the Christmas pageant when I was little. That's why I have issues," he would someday tell his shrink.

But hey, ask me if I care. There are just some things you have to experience in life. Christmas pageants are high on the list in my book.

I had previously hesitated about having our handicapped child Mimi participate, and for good reasons. When she was a baby until about five years old, we carried Mimi in our arms into church every Sunday. She had always been as light as a bag of feathers and sat in my lap. Mimi could not sit alone without falling over. We blended in quite nicely with all the other "normal" families until the day she got too heavy to carry and we decided it was time to bring the wheelchair to church.

Once the decision was made to jump into the pageant arena, I started fretting about how Mimi would behave. What if she reached out and grabbed someone to hug as she was pushed down the aisle in her wheelchair? Hugging people at church has always been one of her favorite hobbies. I also envisioned Mimi waving at everyone in the pews with her "Miss America" wave all the way down the aisle. But if I hesitated another year, it would mean she would be too old to wear those cute yellow poster board angel wings, and then Ricky was not far behind in the age department.

So, I attended the first meeting with Mimi and Ricky in tow. We were committed. I'm not sure how all the parts were cast, but Ricky got shepherd duty, and rightfully so. He'd had his heart set on being one of the wise men.

"Mom, I really wanted to be one of the wise guys. They get to wear the coolest costumes," Ricky told me later.

But the lad was obviously shepherd material. He was born with a gene inherited from dad that is responsible for his wiggling. I understand he will outgrow the trait by the time he is twenty-five. Until then, it is Ricky's destiny to always be a shepherd, and never a king in the Christmas Pageant.

Mimi gladly accepted her angel assignment, which is how we have always thought of her anyway. She was a natural, as were all the cute little girls in the group. The head Pageant chief gave the "angel moms" wing patterns and yellow poster board. Now all I had to do was make the costumes and pray they'd behave.

However, it was soon discovered that Mimi's outfit posed a slight technical problem. We couldn't figure out how to get her wings attached to the angel robe. Her wheelchair was in the way. Finally, after much discussion, my engineering husband came up with a simple solution. It is one of the reasons why I married him. He has always been able to see the obvious when I get lost in the forest. He simply cut a couple of slots in the wings and slid them between the back of her wheelchair and the handles.

The big day came too soon, as I was rushing around minutes before we had to leave gluing gold glitter to Mimi's cardboard wings, and begging Ricky to hold still while dad straightened his headgear. It would be a miracle if his robe stayed on for five minutes. I stood at the back of the church and helped while the kids processed. Except for some minor bumping into the other shepherds, Ricky did fine, although his costume was on the floor by the end of church.

"Too scratchy and hot," was Ricky's excuse.

Mimi was one of the last angels to literally float down the aisle toward the rest of her angelic group. I remain eternally grateful to the oldest angel, who expertly wheeled Mimi, turned her around, and locked her brakes so she couldn't wander. Our little wheelchair angel sat perfectly still with her hands folded in her lap for the entire program. She didn't even lose her halo. I was so proud. Fortunately, someone loaned me a Kleenex when the tears started gushing.

The discussion continues about which Christmas Mass the Frantz family will attend this year. Whichever we chose, it is certain my heart will return momentarily to an earlier time when a wheelchair angel and wiggly shepherd helped in some small way to recreate the story of the birth of our Lord.

—

For many years when the kids were young, we prayed the rosary as a family. Everyone sat on the couch in the family room. Mimi sat in her wheelchair very close to our little rosary circle. Mimi held her own over-sized wooden rosary beads, which were chunky and colorful. Led by her dad, Mimi played with her rosary while the rest of us prayed out loud. Mimi couldn't verbalize the prayers, but she was certainly engaged with us. And just as in church, she didn't hum during the praying of the rosary.

Often, I would look over at her and notice her eyes looking up at the ceiling. Mimi's eyes would light up along with a big smile. Katie also noticed. The two of us speculated afterward. It was as if angels flew above us and Mimi saw them. This was so unusual. Mimi never had a fascination with anything from above, like a light or a ceiling fan. In fact, she rarely looked skyward on our walks. Her eyes were almost always grounded to what appeared in front of her.

Fast-forward a bunch of years. Katie and Ricky grew up. Katie went to college, graduated from graduate school, married, and had babies. Several years after Katie, Ricky went to college, joined the air force, graduated from graduate school, married, and had babies.

Rick and I continued praying the rosary, but after Mimi went to bed. Among many others, our rosary intentions always included keeping Mimi and her friends at the day center safe from harm. After Mimi left us, I asked Rick how Mimi could be taken from us when we had prayed to keep her safe for so many years. I don't know the answer to this question. It still haunts me.

One evening after Mimi had left us, when Rick and I were praying the rosary, I had a revelation while praying the fourth sorrowful mystery, "The Carrying of the Cross." The fruit of the mystery is "patience under crosses." This is the mystery Mimi lived daily. She willingly embraced her cross with a hug each day of her life. The interesting part is, I don't believe she was ever sorrowful about it.

Rick told me he thought that sometimes God asks individuals before they're even born to suffer during their lives for the love of Him. He believes Mimi had said "yes" to God. Her reward is now infinite bliss and happiness in heaven. I believe it also.

When Mimi left us, the same colorful beads she had fingered for years were placed in her niche with her urn.

Mimi practices sitting in her "corner."

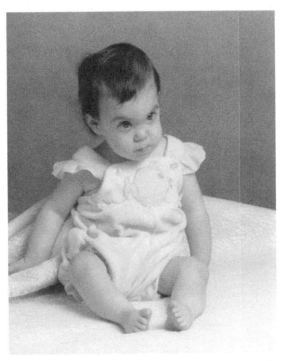

Mimi is 8 months old being held up from behind in this photo.

Handprint quilt from Early Childhood.

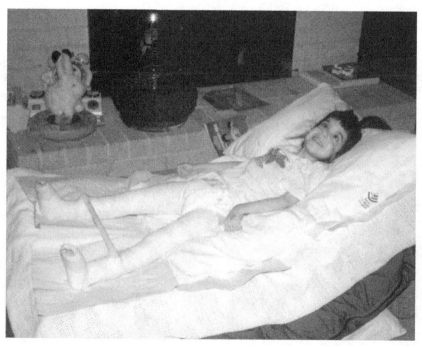

Mimi after hip surgery in body cast.

5/20/91

Mimi works with her physical therapist in Middle School.

A joyful embrace in Ms. Keeling's Class.

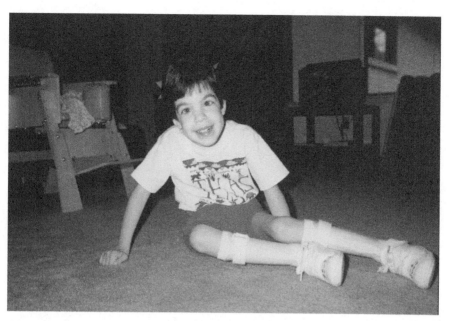

Mimi with her AFO's.

Mimi's First Holy Communion.

PART TWO

Chapter Seven
Mimi's Close Peeps

Let us be grateful to the people who make us happy;
they are the charming gardeners who make our souls blossom.

— Marcel Proust

I like to tell people my husband has nine sisters and a brother and then watch their faces. He grew up in Houston in a large Catholic family, was an altar boy, and attended Catholic school for many years. His mother was very saintly, and his father worked a lot. You can imagine the weekly trips to the day-old bakery and the laundromat.

I never tired of listening to all the funny stories Rick told me over the years about his childhood. One of my favorites is about how sometimes he received a mayonnaise sandwich in his lunch instead of one that included meat and cheese. A couple of his sisters oversaw school lunches, and sometimes their sandwich assembly line process didn't pan out.

Rick lovingly brought me to the Catholic church before we tied the knot. I was just nineteen, and he was twenty-three years old when we married. We were just two kids trying to figure things out. His sense of humor and keen mind are just two of the fine qualities that attracted me to him.

We grew up together, struggling before really beginning our lives. Rick wasn't the best of students, but had the tenacity of a junkyard bulldog. I knew how to type eighty words a minute. We were an interesting combination. I worked, and after a few years, Rick received his engineering degree from The University of Texas at Austin. Earl Campbell played football at the time Rick was at UT. We never had enough money to attend one of his football games, so we admired Earl from afar.

Rick's commitment to Mimi was special. She was always his little girl. Mimi called him "Daddy." The girl really knew how to tug on his heart-strings. Rick dedicated lots of his time and energy to making it easier for Mimi to move around the house, access her surroundings, and be able to do simple things — like take a bath. Rick never saw obstacles where Mimi was concerned — only solutions. We were both caregivers to Mimi, but in very different ways.

—

I'll never forget praying to God after losing our first child to a miscarriage. Afterward, I timidly asked for a girl, with a caveat. I would certainly adore a little boy if that was God's will. But a girl would be oh so fine. Imagine my surprise when Katie was born. She was born ten days past my due date. It was a sweltering Houston summer in 1980, so you can imagine. Lots of days with over-one-hundred-degree temperatures. My ankles, feet, and, heck, even my little toes were beyond swollen. If someone had stuck me with a fork, I would've popped into lots of bits and pieces all over the walls and ceiling. As it was, I had to quit work as a legal secretary a month early.

But my heart was beyond full. Katie was the love of my life, and until Mimi and Ricky were born, I never knew there could be room for more children to love. Isn't it amazing how God makes lots more room in a mother's heart for the second and third child, and so on?

For four years, until Mimi was born, Rick and I doted on Katie, making memories and mistakes as all parents do with their first. But we had laundry-loads of fun! I never wanted her to crawl off the blanket.

Katie is remarkable in my eyes, and to this day is my best friend. We are connected at the soul. We are incredible travel buddies and confidantes. And when we are together, we talk like we haven't seen each other for years.

I feel certain Mimi has influenced Katie's life in a profound way, making her sensitive, deep, and thoughtful. Just like Ricky's, her perspective is unique. But I can't help but think being Mimi's big sister wasn't always easy. Rick and I were the adults. Katie was a small child when Mimi entered our little family. From the day the physical therapist did her first session at our house, I felt so guilty about what that moment and all the rest were doing to Katie. She had to watch week after week as Mimi cried during physical therapy. No amount of explaining to a four-year-old is going to make sense of physical therapy on that level. I feared Katie would be forced to grow up faster than the average firstborn. As I was also the firstborn of five siblings, I could relate a little.

I kept close those many challenging Mimi moments over the years, vowing to do what I could to make it up to Katie. Starting in middle school, I sent her to various academic summer camps. It was usually only for a week at a time, but Katie thrived on learning and was very social. I also flew her to my mom and dad's house in Washington for a couple of weeks during the summer for many years. The summer months were a tad difficult to get through. I reasoned at least Katie would have some interesting experiences that would broaden her horizons.

After high school graduation, Katie went off to college, achieving a bachelor's at The University of Texas at Austin. She held down a part-time job, joined a sorority, and held a leadership position. She also served in the student government. Katie studied abroad for a summer in Italy.

Our favorite mother-daughter adventure happened when Katie finished her program abroad. I met her in Milan for ten days of exploration in 2000. We also traveled to Venice, Florence, and Rome. It was during that time the travel bug bit me big-time. I happily blame my daughter.

Katie also graduated with a master's in humanities from the University of Dallas. For obvious reasons, I like to dub Katie "my very busy daughter."

Several years later, Katie married Chad, one heck of a great guy. As parents, Rick and I pinch ourselves. We will never have to worry about those two. They have two great little boys named Jacob and Ben. It is my greatest joy to spoil them like a bag of rotten tomatoes. Katie and Chad's Saturday family excursions around Houston and beyond are legendary.

—

Lots of people thought Mimi was our youngest child. Not so. There are three years between Ricky and Mimi. Ricky is our youngest child, born in 1987.

But I like to say … not really our youngest. I have told a few people the story about his unusual birth. But there is a backstory. Rick and I were at a time in our lives when he had the college degree, we had the house, the dog, and the fenced yard. Babies were next on the list, and I wanted one born during the month of May. When I miscarried at almost three months, we were devastated. One day there was a heartbeat — and then there was not. It was a very humbling experience. I foolishly thought I was in control. I soon learned, and over the years relearned many times, God was the one in control.

It took me a little longer than expected to get pregnant a second time. When Katie was born in 1980 and total bliss set in, I kept that little miscarried angel we lost in a special place in my heart.

—

After Mimi was born in 1984, I thought our family was complete and our hands plenty full. But again, God had other plans. I wish I had a picture of the look on my face when the doctor told me we were expecting a third baby — and that little bundle would be born in May. Ricky weighed nine pounds and nine ounces when he was born on May 6, a few days after my thirty-fourth birthday. What a gift. You see, I believe our little miscarried angel flew around in heaven for a bunch of years before being born in May. What could be the reason for him weighing so much? Obviously, he was putting on pounds while waiting long enough to be born.

With just three years between them, Mimi and Ricky had an interesting relationship. Mimi couldn't enunciate "Ricky." She called him "Re-Re." I think Mimi understood from the very beginning that she was the older sister, and she treated him that way. For a long time, I carted the two of them around in a double stroller. That is, until Ricky grew too wide for it.

From the moment Ricky started crawling around the house, Mimi started following him to see what he was up to. She loved to watch. Her mode of transportation was combat crawling. Mimi never could get her body up on her knees to crawl. Her hips were too unstable. Instead, she used her forearms to propel herself forward, dragging the rest of her body behind her.

Ricky didn't seem to notice his sister was different. By this time, Mimi was receiving therapy at school. He took Mimi's surgeries in stride. This tough stuff for his parents was normal for him. Just like Katie, Ricky joined in on keeping Mimi happy and distracted during those tough orthopedic body cast weeks.

Ricky was always the first to launch a wadded-up napkin across the dinner table in Mimi's direction. I think he enjoyed her cackling reaction.

Ricky received his bachelor's degree from Virginia Military Institute. He studied abroad in Spain for one semester. Ricky also has a couple of master's degrees, including one from George Mason University in Washington, DC, in cyber security. He serves his country as a major in the air force, as he likes to say, "spreading the blanket of freedom each day." He is married to the lovely Kate, and they have two young daughters, Zelie and Melanie. Melanie is named in honor of his little sister. Grandson Leo was born in late 2022.

—

I learned everything I needed to know about being a mother from my mom. She was born in Holland in 1933. She was the youngest of six siblings, with five older brothers, including a pair of twins. Her father was a tenant farmer, milking cows and taking care of the water levels using a windmill. Her mother had lots of health problems that began after the birth of the twins.

My mother was seven years old when World War II broke out. She doesn't recall what life was like before the Nazi occupation of the Netherlands began in 1940. Her oldest brother, Jan, died in a German work camp near the very end of the war. Her father, mother, one brother, and she emigrated to America, passing through Ellis Island in 1948. They were sponsored by my mom's uncle and came to California to live and work. Her remaining brothers came to America a few years later.

Prompted by my mother's childhood stories about growing up in Holland, my sister and I have performed additional research and, separately, visited Holland. My sister, Mary, tragically died a few years back from ovarian cancer. I was gifted with her research after Mary left us. I hope to write a book about my mother and her family's life of sorrow and survival. It is quite a story.

My mom and dad had five children: three girls and two boys. My mother joyfully raised us and loved every minute of it. Considering her unique childhood, family meant everything to her. She continues to be an important part of Katie's, Mimi's, and Ricky's lives.

—

Gretchen is my little sister. We are six years apart in age. We have lived far from each other more than half our lives, but are tethered with long, invisible strings at the heart.

Whenever Mimi received something in the mail, I would ask her something like, "Who do you think this is from?" She always said "Gretchen" in her own Mimi lingo. Obviously, my sister's love language is gifts. She loves to give them and is very good at figuring out what to give!

Mimi's favorite gift from her Aunt Gretchen was a "gumball" machine for M&M's. It is covered with lots of colorful stickers on the outside, with *Sesame Street* characters and words like "hands off" and "yum yum." It sat on her dresser for years. All Mimi had to do was point at it and I would put several in my hand for her to sample while she watched her favorite television game show.

Up until the day Mimi left us, our grandsons, Jacob and Ben, used to love to head to Mimi's room and raid the M&M's machine. Several times I would find a bunch of the candy on the carpet in front of the dresser. It dispenses from beneath the bowl, but we let the batteries wear out on purpose. Makes it harder to retrieve a handful from the opening on top.

Keeping the legacy alive, and as the kids' love of M&M's endures, we moved the dispenser to a higher level. The M&M's dispenser now sits on the kitchen counter. After obligatory hugs, Jacob and Ben grab a red plastic cup from the pantry and ask for a bit of their favorite treat. The colorful contents are a constant reminder of an aunt's love for her niece.

—

Sometimes favorite peeps come with four furry paws. When Mimi was little, we had this adorable cocker spaniel whose name was Peaches 'n

Cream, also known as Peaches, or, as Mimi called her, Pee-Wee. Pee-Wee had a beautiful light peach coat and very gentle nature. Peaches never learned to retrieve the newspaper or "stay" on command. In fact, if Pee-Wee escaped out the front door, we wouldn't see her back at our house until she had eaten all the cat food in the neighborhood. We knew this to be true as the contents of our dog's tummy often ended up on the carpet sometime after her return.

Peaches adored Mimi. They were huge pals. Back then I would put a fluffy quilt on the carpet and set Mimi on her stomach in front of the television. That is where she would watch her favorite show while I was fixing dinner. Peaches would always hang out nearby.

Sometime between finishing dinner and setting the table, I would place a scoop of dry dog food in Peaches' bowl in the kitchen. The dog had this interesting habit that always made me smile. Peaches would pick up in her mouth just one of the small dog food morsels and bring it over to where Mimi was watching her show. Peaches would then drop it on the quilt near Mimi and step back to wait. The first time Peaches brought the morsel to Mimi, I happened to be peeking around the corner. My first reaction was, oh no! I thought Mimi was going to put it in her own mouth thinking it was an M&M or some other food. I feel certain children have eaten dog food for decades, but Mimi wasn't going to be one of them if I could help it. Mimi picked up the morsel and gently pitched it with her left hand toward Peaches, as if to say, "Yep, it is okay to eat your food now. I approve." I never tired of watching their adorable little exchange.

Did I mention Peaches had a congenital heart murmur? The vet told us there was nothing that could be done, and it would probably just shorten her life a few years. In 2000, Pee-Wee died suddenly. I feel certain Mimi did not understand death. But Mimi certainly noticed Peaches was gone. Whenever Mimi would say Pee-Wee's name, I would always tell her Peaches went to puppy heaven. My slightly sad face reflected that we were sad about that, and I guess Mimi took it to her tender heart. Many years later, when she met someone, Mimi would say "Pee-Wee awwww." It was Mimi's way to let everyone know she was still thinking about her puppy in heaven and wanted you to know it.

Chapter Eight

Awkward Middle School Years

What matters most is how well
you walk through the fire.

– Charles Bukowski

Let's face it. The middle school years are difficult for children even without a disability or two or three in the mix. Ask any adult if they would like to go back to those awkward years, and most will run for the door with the Exit sign. It was not any different for Mimi. Although she seemed much more relaxed and easygoing about middle school than I was.

It was still challenging to communicate with Mimi. That was a given, despite years of observation and my forever trying to insert myself into her head and soul. It had given me a better understanding of who Mimi was than anyone on the planet. By middle school, Mimi was so used to our daily routines, she would often finish my sentences with a single word.

For instance, each morning before school, she would be scooping her cut-up pancakes with a spoon and drinking her milk. I would sit near her with the daily newspaper. Mimi would look at me and say, "peek." I guess years of referring to my reading the paper as "I am going to just peek at the paper" paid off.

Katie compared the relationship Mimi and I had to a Venn diagram. Imagine two circles. One is Mimi, and the other — me. Then bring the two circles close together and overlap them. Katie was right. I was a part of Mimi and she was a part of me. It was the perfect analogy.

But Mimi's lack of verbal communication made it tough for teachers to plug into her. I recall a semester when a teacher commented Mimi "had not said a word for weeks." Mimi preferred to observe, especially if no one was specifically engaging her. Unfortunately, Mimi had one middle school teacher who decided to focus on Mimi's perceived body language and got it all very wrong.

—

I could appreciate where the teacher was coming from when I received a disturbing entry in Mimi's spiral notebook. The teacher let me know Mimi was touching her chest in a sexual way, especially when a male teacher was nearby. I knew exactly the behavior she was referring to. Mimi was happy and excited when familiar people came near her. When someone spoke to her, Mimi got excited and would slap her chest with one hand and then put her arms up for a hug.

Since the teachers and aides in her class were not allowing hugging, as her IEP mandated, Mimi would engage any adult outside the classroom. I explained these details to the teacher and quickly reminded her that Mimi was mentally a two-year-old. I should not have had to tell her that factoid. I felt strongly the teacher should not be focusing on Mimi's body language in that way.

The teacher then wrote back about her complete disagreement. She told me the feelings Mimi had were normal for middle schoolers and Mimi's "touching" herself was certainly sexual. We did our back and forth in the spiral notebook for several notebook entries. Sometimes the teacher seemed to let it go. I wouldn't receive anything about Mimi's supposed behavior.

Then a week later it would come up again. Finally, I suggested a conference with her and the principal. This was getting out of hand.

It was that whole Pandora's box story, with a new evil inserting itself in Mimi's life. My fear was the teacher would talk about this with other staff members and attach another label to our daughter. Of course, it was an issue where the big guns — Mimi's daddy — were needed. Rick and I very strongly explained to the teacher, in the presence of the principal, who exactly Mimi was, and that the teacher needed to immediately get off her sexual soap box. Yes, Mimi was indeed slapping her hand on her chest. But her hand did not in any way linger or rub. The teacher finally agreed to move on.

I never had another teacher or staff member ever suggest during the rest of middle school, high school, or at the adult day center that Mimi was touching her chest in a sexual way. That episode in middle school was a bizarre time for us, but it wasn't the last.

—

Then there was another entry that caught my eye in Mimi's spiral notebook. The teacher indicated Mimi was put into a time-out for throwing crayons. This was very puzzling to me. While Mimi could be stubborn and manipulative, this was her very first time-out in school. She had never had one at home.

The next day, I asked the teacher, via spiral notebook, for a few more details. The incident seemed very odd to me. Let me set the stage. In elementary school, there was lots of instruction with students in a circle on the floor. It seems in middle school, the life skills students sat at desks and worked on papers for part of the school day.

Mimi had never used her hands much. She couldn't, and coloring was extremely difficult. It didn't mean we didn't encourage Mimi to use her hands. For me, Mimi would attempt only a couple of scribbles in a coloring book. That would last two seconds at best, and she was done.

I could see how her crayon might naturally roll to the floor after use. Perhaps I could even see her gently toss a crayon. Mostly, she would just transfer a crayon from hand to hand. I could not see a time-out being of any value and wrote the teacher as much. I also mentioned my appreciation for her trying to discipline Mimi, but added it probably wouldn't work.

Katie and Ricky thought it was funny that Mimi was put in a time-out. They had their share of punishments over the years and believed it was past time for Mimi to have the same experience.

I discussed the time-out with the bus driver who picked Mimi up the following day. She had a much different perspective. Her son attended a school for the blind in Austin. He stayed at the school during the week and came home on the weekends. When he was thirteen, he had an altercation with a girl at school who swung her backpack at him and missed. Actually, I believe there was a little middle school flirting going on. The girl was completely blind, while the driver's son had enough vision to swing his backpack and hit his mark. The bus driver compared her son's vision to what one might see looking through a straw. The minor incident sparked a phone call home. Her son was suspended for one day for fighting. There was zero tolerance at the school. The school had strict rules. This meant the bus driver had to drive over three hours to Austin to pick her son up. Yikes!

The bus driver believed Mimi's time-out was a developmental milestone and should be celebrated. I was beyond puzzled, but gradually came to appreciate her interesting point of view. Yep, Mimi's first time-out was indeed a strange and wonderful developmental milestone. I really should include that little tidbit in her baby book in large letters!

—

Middle school continued to present challenging issues. Let me first state the obvious. The world is definitely not flat like a pancake. Families with a loved one in a wheelchair know this better than most people. There are curbs, single steps, and lots of stairs most everywhere you wander. Thank you, Jesus, for elevators and ramps and flat places!

Still, I was surprised when I received a telephone call from the middle school one afternoon. Mimi was in the nurse's office, though I was immediately told she was fine. It was my first clue I wasn't going to like the next thing the nurse had to say. It seems Mimi and her wheelchair were being pushed after theater arts class by a substitute aide who wasn't paying attention to a steep drop-off. Mimi and her wheelchair went over on one side. I can't even imagine being in that room when it happened. The wheelchair was quickly righted. Mimi was fine, although plenty of tears flowed. Thankfully, her arm and hand were close to her body when the chair tipped over, or there would have been lots of broken bones.

Of course, when something like this happens, there needs to be an immediate response. I feel certain the principal hated to see us in his office again so soon. We talked about safety and who was allowed control of Mimi's wheelchair. There was some ranting and raving, but nothing that got terribly out of control ... much. In moments like these, I agonized if I should ever let Mimi out into the world at all.

This wasn't the last time Mimi had an accident in middle school. Once, an aide was pushing Mimi's wheelchair and was distracted. After reviewing exactly what happened, the school told us the aide was approaching a ramp rather quickly, and Mimi reached down to stop the wheelchair from moving. Apparently, Mimi was feeling unstable, like she was going to fall. The aide didn't notice and kept moving. One of Mimi's hands was caught in the wheelchair's brake. The aide stopped when Mimi cried out. Her little hand did not require stitches, but it was certainly a bloody mess, and this was a preventable accident.

Each time Mimi was hurt, I would agonize over wanting to just keep her in our house forever and protect her, not send her to school, and not go out into the community. It seemed that when she was at home, at least I could protect her from the outside world. There was a tension between me wanting to protect Mimi and keep her home and realizing I had to let her experience the world. It was a difficult dilemma.

My resolution, after a few tears, was scheduling another meeting with the principal and the teacher to figure out how to make Mimi's world safer. But are protocols and rules enough to accomplish those goals? I felt I had done everything I could do, but it didn't feel like enough.

—

It wasn't long until middle school for Mimi was about to have another hiccup. In the late '80s and early '90s, inclusion for special education students started to be a big thing. I am not certain how inclusion is accomplished now, but for Mimi it was a challenge in middle school. For most life skills students, it had to be more of a challenge. In Mimi's case, there was no way they could include her in an English, history, or math class. According to the ARD meeting I attended the year before the new school year, electives were often the best fit. I agreed. They recommended a music class. Mimi certainly had no singing ability, but boy could she hum. It was more like one long, loud note! The academic members of the ARD meeting convinced me the music class was appropriate for Mimi.

I learned the class was more like beginning choir. I don't know why I thought it was more like music appreciation. I knew there were a couple of other students with special needs who also attended the class with Mimi, along with an aide. One day, I became curious and asked to sit in on the class. About twenty or thirty students were singing with their instructor. Mimi and those with special needs sat silent, far apart, with a classroom aide. It did not take me long to decide this was not where Mimi needed to be. If Mimi started humming, it would be disruptive. If she sat there silent, there was no inclusion going on. When we started planning for the next semester, the music class was crossed off my list for Mimi. What a waste of a semester. If I had had a discussion with the ARD committee about why they thought the music class would benefit Mimi, I might have had better information and suggested a more appropriate elective.

—

After the fiasco with the music class, Mimi was assigned to theater arts in the fall. I had no preconceived notions theater was going to be any better than music. But there was hope. I had heard through Mimi's teacher that the life skills students were embraced and actually participated in the class. I just wanted it to be a positive experience for Mimi and the rest of the class.

Late in the semester, parents were invited by the theater arts teacher to see what was going on in the class. It was during the school day, and they were going to be putting on a little play. Imagine my surprise when a little musical skit with creative strobe lighting was performed, and Mimi was in the middle of the stage with a group of students on both sides. All Mimi had to do was wave her arms around to the music, and she did. Everyone looked like they were having so much fun on stage, including Mimi.

Occasionally, I would receive a little note about how much the theater arts teacher enjoyed having Mimi in her class. Made me cry buckets of tears every time. Mimi's inclusion class remained theater arts for the remainder of her time in middle school.

—

It was toward the end of Mimi's third year of middle school that a certain pressure was being applied in our direction. I will never forget the diagnostician gingerly suggesting Mimi transition from middle school to high school.

In my mind, since most special education students are usually in public school until they age out at twenty-two, there was nothing magical about age as far as advancing from grade to grade for Mimi. She just was either in early childhood, elementary, middle, or high school.

When the idea was floated that Mimi should transition to high school, I panicked. I calculated she would be spending six years in high school if she transitioned when it was suggested. We went round and round the table until finally someone, I think it was one of the therapists, suggested I go to the high school and observe. I didn't know that was an option. We tabled the ARD. I arranged to visit the high school program and to observe the class and meet the teacher and aide.

The observation was very enlightening. I loved the teacher and aide. There was no issue with them. In fact, I looked forward to Mimi being in their life skills program. At the time of my observation, there were only two students in the class. They were also nonverbal and hardly moved. My heart hurt for them and their parents. But I would have loved for Mimi to be in a classroom where there was some verbal interaction with her peers. Mimi had increased her vocabulary in middle school. I deemed this was due to her interaction with her life skills peers and the regular students through inclusion. It would be nice to continue that trend. Unfortunately, I knew there would be fewer and fewer opportunities for inclusion with the regular school population in high school.

The high school teacher, Ms. Peggy, would have loved to have Mimi in the fall, but understood my concern. Based on her meetings at the middle school ARDs, she suggested Mimi wait a year before entering high school. There were several other students who would come up with Mimi at that time, and they were somewhat verbal. Also, Ms. Peggy mentioned they had a teacher who taught a fun shop class that was modified for the life skills class.

I left with the answer as to where Mimi best fit. She should wait one year before heading to high school. When Mimi's ARD meeting was reconvened, everyone agreed — one of them reluctantly.

In 2013, I wrote a column for *The Tribune* about an interesting conversation with a classroom aide in the high school class after Mimi transitioned to high school.

The Tribune
You Gotta Laugh — "It Is a Lot Like Eating Liver"
Written by Dixie Frantz
Published July 31, 2013

Did you ever meet a person that REALLY LOVES what they do for a living? I have. Well, I don't literally high-five one every day, but it does happen a lot. For me, this time of year it occurs way more often than a light blue, hot pink or even a lightly yellow-tinted moon made entirely out of Swiss cheese.

I will never forget the day I had the epiphany. It came from a simple comment via a classroom aide when our special needs daughter was in high school. About ten years ago I was helping out with a classroom party. There was some downtime between serving cake and cleaning up. Yep, and when that happens it is a sure thing my motor mouth will start running like a Corvette Stingray lap car, flat out, pedal to the metal in first gear. Obviously, I am not especially shy.

I don't recall how the two of us got on the subject of jobs. Probably started out with me commenting how much I admired her and what a difficult one she had helping the teacher with all the various needs in the classroom. Some of the students in this particular special needs class were a handful. What the aide said next has obviously stuck to one of my especially large brain cells all these years.

"You know ... working in special education is a lot like eating liver. The first time you eat it ... (pregnant pause) ... you either love it ... or you hate it. There is no in between," she said with a big smile.

Obviously, she was a lover of liver in all its forms: chopped, deep-fried, pate, foie gras and my husband's personal fave when he was a kid ... just plain old liver and onions!

It's like that with any profession really. You know it when you meet someone passionate about what they do. That little "liver comment" has made me smile many times over the years. I'm talkin' about all the awesome people that have touched Mimi's life: an amazing pediatrician that still has lunch with us once a year, physical therapists, speech therapists, occupational therapists, teachers, bus drivers, one particular diagnostician and a pretty amazing principal that actually knew all the names of his special needs students in high school.

While liver is definitely not on the menu at the Frantz house, my thoughts travel there today and I smile. At present I am gearing up for packing Mimi's stuff before heading off for five fun-filled days at summer camp near Brenham. It usually takes me a whole Saturday to get everything just right. Stuff like marking any new item with permanent marker and locating the rain poncho that has never been used. This just could be the year when it rains buckets! Oh, and the hot pink twin sheets. I bought them for Mimi a few years back to make a summer camp fashion statement. They are in a closet somewhere. And I'll be in major trouble if I forget the long pants for Mimi's favorite camp activity ... horseback riding.

It is during days like packing for camp that I reflect on all the awesome staff it takes to put on a camp for those with special needs. People who probably won't get but a few hours sleep a night and yet be so jazzed about getting a camper ready for the zip line. I always worry if Mimi will get that right buddy to do the little things like brush her teeth and coax her to eat that last bite of a meal. Mimi would rather socialize then eat.

Yep, every year I am so humbled that I can be replaced so adequately for 5 days with passionate people that obviously love liver!

Chapter Nine

Child Protective Services Comes Knocking

At any given moment you have the power to say:
this is not how the story is going to end.

– Christine Mason Miller

I need to put in a disclaimer for this chapter. What you are about to read is graphic and disturbing on so many levels.

Maybe you have read newspaper stories about Child Protective Services (CPS) coming to pick up an allegedly neglected child from a home littered with garbage. Horrible nightmares indeed for that poor child, and certainly a good reason to have a safety net for abused children. CPS has its place for these children.

However, families with special needs children should be aware of the power of CPS. I think in many cases social workers have not come across children with special needs. CPS has unbelievable power. They can take your special child away, and the minor children in your family. This is a cautionary tale of what can happen when CPS comes knocking at your door.

Mimi was attending another six weeks of summer school as part of her life skills program at a school campus over thirty minutes from our house. Each morning, I put Mimi on the school bus. With this program, Mimi returned before lunchtime.

Through the spiral notebook that hung out in Mimi's wheelchair backpack, the teacher and I wrote long notes back and forth each day. Every single one of those notes was positive on both sides. For Mimi's birthday in mid-July, I sent homemade cookies with festive paper plates and napkins for the class and the teacher to share. With two other children at home, I used the few hours Mimi was at school to run errands and attack housework with a vengeance. I never appeared in person at the school during the summer session. I never appeared at any of the previous years' summer programs. It was my thought to not interfere with the few hours of instruction going on in the classroom. I figured everything was said via the spiral notebook, and if there was an issue, a phone call or a visit would indeed be in order. There was never any indication of any issue until the last day of the program.

I still have the spiral notebook from that summer program. I will never throw it away. As I read through it even today, the positive comments are stunning.

But let me back up to the last day of summer school. I was busy packing Mimi's clothes for the big drive to summer camp the next day when the telephone rang. It was Mimi's teacher. She asked me if I noticed Mimi had a white discharge from her vagina when I changed Mimi's pull-up. I indicated that I had noticed. It was normal. I had spoken with our pediatrician about it on one occasion. Mimi had started her period a year or so earlier, just like most every other young lady. I next spoke two little words that would seal my fate and drag our family down into a deep, dark abyss.

"Duly noted," I said.

I was so busy packing for summer camp, I didn't realize how those last two words before we hung up the phone would be misinterpreted. Mimi returned home happy on the little school bus, with no hint at what had transpired after our phone conversation.

I didn't think about the call again until a week after Mimi returned from a great five days of summer camp. There was a knock on our door. I opened it to find a lady representing CPS who wanted to come in and ask some questions. She also wanted to interview Mimi.

A few words about what happens when you ask Mimi questions. Remember, Mimi was intellectually a delightful two-year-old, but with a twist. If you asked her a "yes/no" question with a happy inflection in your voice, Mimi would answer any question with a "yeah," and a cute little smile. It did not matter if you asked Mimi if she wanted to eat yucky broccoli, jump off a cliff, or go to McDonald's. That would be her answer.

If you asked Mimi a question with a pouty, sad inflection, she might cry. Often, Mimi would shake her head and say "mo," which means no. When the CPS lady asked to interview Mimi, I started to panic.

My husband didn't take the CPS lady coming into our house very well. In fact, he was upset and let her know it. The lady let Rick know she could take Mimi and Ricky, who was still a minor child, into her custody if we did not cooperate. I ordered Rick to the back yard to cool off. The situation was quickly spinning out of control.

In talking to CPS, I learned a little about why she was in our house. She told me CPS had received a call that Mimi might have been sexually abused because of the presence of a white discharge in her pull-up she believed was semen. I immediately knew she was talking about the last day of summer school and the phone call. The CPS lady also let me know the name of the person reporting was confidential.

After Rick kind of apologized, the lady ordered us to report to Houston's CPS office the next day, and to bring all our children, for an interview. She also mentioned Mimi would be examined by a doctor at CPS for signs of abuse.

I knew someone in law enforcement and called to ask his advice on what to do. We didn't know if we should engage an attorney. After speaking to our friend, it was decided we would not engage an attorney. The facts would speak for themselves. We believed it was a misunderstanding and nothing more.

But I also didn't like that CPS would be examining Mimi in such a personal way. Can you imagine? I also learned I was not going to be able to be with Mimi during this intimate examination. With all Mimi's orthopedic challenges, like tight hips, the kind of examination CPS would want to perform made us all very upset. I called our pediatrician and asked if I could get CPS to let him examine Mimi, would he agree to report his findings? He stated he would. Now I just had to get CPS to agree.

Then, Rick had to explain to Ricky what was going on. Imagine explaining to your young son he was going to be interviewed by some grownups he did not know and asked if he had ever abused his sister.

Our drive down to CPS in Houston was emotionally dark. We didn't know what to expect and feared a negative outcome. I brought along one of Mimi's favorite stuffed animals for her to hold. As we all waited in the reception area, someone came in and offered Mimi a stuffed animal. Mimi held on to the one brought from home.

We were all interviewed individually, except for Mimi. After getting a clearer picture of our family, they finally lightened up. CPS figured out Mimi was not able to accurately answer questions. But they still wanted to examine Mimi. I respectfully asked if we could use our own pediatrician in place of the examination by their doctor. After leaving all of us in the waiting room for what seemed like hours, they agreed it would be fine. They would wait to hear from Mimi's pediatrician and generate a formal report.

Eventually, we learned someone (a teacher and/or an aide in the summer school program) had asked Mimi a question about being abused that she couldn't possibly have answered with the words recorded in the report. Someone had basically put words into Mimi's mouth. CPS agreed Mimi was clearly not able to answer questions. The investigation had nothing to do with her little brother, father, sister, or mother, or even the janitor at the school. Sadly, CPS's conclusion was it had to do with Mimi's lack of understanding and her lack of communication skills. This was the day I fully realized Mimi was one of the most vulnerable in our society. Protecting Mimi from the outside world was becoming a full-time job. These incidents made my chest hurt sometimes, like perpetual heartburn that rarely goes away. On the other hand, thankfully, Mimi never seemed to realize all the hurtful things that were swirling around her.

We were verbally told the outcome of the CPS report. I made sure to keep in touch with CPS as to when the report would be finally issued. We were told the report would be expunged, but I wanted to read for myself what was in the report. I picked up the copy many weeks after the event and read every single page. The report was eighty double-spaced pages. Nowhere in the report was there a mention of keeping the pull-up for testing. There was no mention that the school staff put Mimi on the bus home on the last day of summer school. If they really thought Mimi was sexually abused, they should have immediately called the police.

I have an extreme amount of guilt for not stopping my summer camp packing and driving down to the school when the teacher called me that fateful day. I regret saying those two words that probably set the call to CPS in motion.

The CPS report did not mention the teacher lied when quoting words Mimi was not able to articulate. I thought this was very unfair. The teacher made a huge mistake. I made a huge mistake. Just as in the Greek myth, the whole CPS encounter felt as if one of the evils that escaped Pandora's box oddly chose to pay a visit to our family.

We could have paid dearly for the CPS encounter. In their report, CPS could have decided Mimi had been abused. She and Ricky could have been taken away from us. Also, in a few years, we were facing filing for guardianship of Mimi in court. Having a negative report or any kind of CPS filing in her file would have been devastating. Trying to be diligent about all the details in Mimi's life outside of our home was exhausting.

Chapter Ten
It's a Wonderful Life

If you enjoy living, it is not difficult
to keep the sense of wonder.

– Ray Bradbury

Our son, Ricky, was a Cub Scout many moons ago. He participated in the usual scouting activities like pinewood derby racing, camping, fundraising, and working on badges for his Order of the Arrow.

I recall volunteering to drive some of the scouts to a local nursing home to sing Christmas carols. Of course, Mimi went along for the ride. After school, where I went, Mimi went. The elderly residents were all assembled in a large room by the time of our arrival. While the scouts headed to the other side of the room to sing their little hearts out, Mimi and I found a spot in the back. The Christmas mini-concert was delightful. I mean, who doesn't smile at the thought of a bunch of cute little scouts singing in public?

What most surprised me was not the singing from the adorable off-key Cub Scouts. It was the reaction when the elderly residents laid eyes on Mimi. As the residents wheeled past her after the event, many of them touched Mimi and smiled. And Mimi smiled her biggest smile back. The residents had a much different reaction to the rowdy and adorable scouts. Oh, they loved the concert. But there was a tenderness in their eyes over Mimi's presence. Not pity though. Many of the residents were sitting in wheelchairs. I imagined they felt a connection to Mimi, who was probably eleven at the time. Despite her being in a wheelchair, her long, thick black hair, tied in a ponytail with a large red bow, and her big blue eyes presented the picture of health. Quite the opposite of what the residents were experiencing in their lives.

—

I also recall the year Ricky played on a softball team. He was probably seven or eight. As parents, we were encouraging Ricky to try new things. He played soccer, baseball, and eventually tried his hands and feet at tae kwon do. After several years, Ricky achieved his black belt and then calmly announced to his parents, "I'm done."

It was during his time on the baseball team that Ricky hung way out in the outfield, mostly plucking petals off wildflowers. It was not his thing, but he gave it a try for a season.

Of course, Mimi went with me to all the practices and games. Again, where I went, Mimi went. At the end of the season, all the boys received trophies, and the coach said a few kind words about each member of the team. All the boys had come such a long way in developing teamwork and baseball skills. I recall how much pride I experienced when Ricky received his trophy. The little guy had progressed from picking flowers and pulling petals to paying attention to what was happening at home plate.

In 2000, I wrote the following column for *The Observer* about a touching baseball experience that revolved around Ricky and Mimi.

The Observer
You Gotta Laugh —
"Scoring a Home Run in the Game of Life"
Written by Dixie Frantz
Published June 7, 2000

There's nothin' like that proud feelin' a parent gets deep down inside between their liver and gall bladder when their kid catches an impossible fly ball, slides into second for a steal, or spits sunflower seeds out the window on the way home from a winning game. Gosh, it is difficult to explain, but there is just something magical about baseball. Our thirteen-year-old son just recently finished up the season playing with a local Pony League and guess I am still having flashbacks. Heck, the family truckster still wants to turn right at the duck pond and head for field three or the batting cages most evenings.

Ricky's previous experience on an organized baseball team was pretty much a disaster when he was in the first grade. I remember it well, or should I say ... not so well, if you know what I mean. Early in the season he had the opportunity to try his glove at the catcher position. Ricky was beaned with the first pitch, a faster-than-lightning-ball to the right kneecap. The kid promptly rolled himself up into a fetal position right there on home plate. That fatalistic pitch sealed his fate and the word "catcher" was stricken from his vocabulary.

"No way you are getting me to play that position again ... and I'm seriously re-thinking this whole baseball thing," was the youngster's reply when the subject was even casually mentioned. He spent the rest of the season in the outfield digging in the dirt with a stick and picking petals off dandelions. I guess he musta felt safe out there and willing to wait out the season communing with nature.

Multiple years passed since the "infamous catcher incident" and then last year, we signed up our handicapped daughter to play on a

*YMCA baseball team for special kids. Her team was called the Green
Gators. Whole families, as well as special education teachers and other
volunteers, came out to help the kids play depending on their individual
needs. We had a couple of kids in wheelchairs, one with a walker, and
lots of great kiddos with various other challenges.*

*Ricky stepped up to the plate to help his sister when it was her turn
to bat. He'd place his hands over Mimi's and the bat, strike the ball
together as it blazed toward them, and then push her wheelchair round
the bases. It was like no other baseball game I'd ever seen before with
parents and kids in the outfield encouraging the player that was "up" to
go for a home run. We only had two teams of special kids, so we played
each other every week that season. And by the time each game was over,
no one knew who had won, or cared. Mimi received her first trophy as a
result of playing with the Gators. Considering she'd been a teenager for
a couple of years, it was a really big deal.*

*It's probably why our son jumped at the chance to play when dad
mentioned "baseball" this spring with Ricky in mind. I have to say that
I feel like a seasoned mom after the whole baseball experience. Just ask
me anything ya want to know about the parts of the uniform from the
name of those boxer things they wear under their baseball pants, to the
gauge of steel for the "cup."*

*The Marlins played a bunch of games and won some of them and
lost some. And under the expert and patient coaching of Jerry, all the
players' skills improved with each game. Mimi and I made all the early
evening games cheering her brother and the team on.*

*Then just when I thought the season was kaput, we ratcheted things
up a notch to play all the teams in our division for something called a
"double elimination" tournament. It turned out to be the most fun of the
season for this mom, who by then, knew the names of the boys on the
team, the difference between hand motions for "you're out" and "safe,"*

and finally managed to remember to bring that disgusting blue-colored drink Ricky likes for the dugout.

In the end, our team placed a most respectable second in their division and received trophies on the field before the first place Braves. Coach Jerry said some very nice words about each boy that evening. But the drama that followed touched more than a few hearts.

Seems there was an extra trophy sitting in the box after the presentations and handshaking. Mimi was asked to join the boys back behind the dugout where they were chowing down on hot dogs and sipping drinks. The coach again said some nice words, but this time about Mimi and her support of the team before presenting her with the extra trophy. It is my official testimony that she was the only trophy recipient to "Grizzly Bear hug" the coach.

Yep, there are many reasons why I like baseball so much. It is a sport with a multitude of interesting hand signals, unique apparel, infinite surprises and people with lots of heart.

—

I would have never sent Mimi to summer camp if it had not been for Stacey. I met Stacey when I was a member of the parent group in the school district. We all had children with special needs. Stacey was the one who encouraged me to consider sending Mimi to Camp CAMP (it stands for Children's Association for Maximum Potential). She said it would be great for Mimi and for me. At one of our meetings, she handed me one of their brochures. I remember sitting on it for a year. Stacey encouraged me the following year, and I finally swallowed the bait. The next year when I mailed off the application, attachments, and payment, I soon had second and third thoughts about what I had done. Stacey kept emotionally pumping me up, saying it would be a great experience.

The first time Mimi went to summer camp, she was about eight years old. I know ... she was so young, right? Camp CAMP is in Center Point, Texas, near Kerrville in the Hill Country. The drive was four and a half hours each way. What a special place. But very rustic. In the early '90s, it was the only camp that would take a child like Mimi who required lots of attention and her own buddy. Back then, there were summer camps for those with special needs, but the campers had to have lots of self-help skills. Mimi couldn't brush her teeth or feed herself, and that was just for starters.

Camp CAMP was started by a group of air force pediatricians in 1979. They solicit as volunteers local high school students from the San Antonio area who are interested in the medical field. Doctors and therapists are also in attendance, to learn and work with special needs campers, but as kids, not as numbers on a chart. The therapists do things like get these kids in the pool and work with them.

Outside of camp, I could always tell when Mimi had a doctor who had experience at a summer camp like this. They always treated Mimi differently. It was more about her quality of life than what kind of surgery a doctor thought she might need. It was a much different approach.

Did I mention the camp was rustic? Let me explain. The camp had air-conditioning in the infirmary, where the most fragile of the special needs campers spent their entire camp days and nights. Campers like Mimi had "swamp coolers" in their cabins. A swamp cooler uses moisture to cool the air by taking warm outside air through wet evaporative cooler pads, effectively cooling the air. Swamp coolers were cheaper than air-conditioning and lowered the temperatures at night.

Back then, their sidewalks were cracked in lots of places, but the camp made it work. The campers enjoyed canoeing, horseback riding, crafts, swimming, games, and so much more. I only know this because I sent a disposable camera with Mimi each year. Mimi could not tell me what she did the five days at camp. She brought back a little booklet that her counselor filled out, which gave me the highlights of the whole camp experience.

The first summer Mimi attended, I remember sitting in a gazebo with another mom. She had a child who had been coming to the camp since he was five. We were waiting to head to the infirmary for Mimi's and the little boy's check-in process. The mom told me he had lots of special needs and loved coming to camp.

I always cried when I dropped Mimi off. The first summer camp was the hardest. I called their main phone number once and the person on the other side assured me our daughter was still among the living. And then every year I would cry when I picked Mimi up. It was so great to get her back. The whole time we were apart, I felt like I was missing my right arm. But Mimi loved going to camp. I soon learned it was her time to shine. Mimi always knew that when we started talking about the month of July, which was also her birthday month, it was time to "pack" for summer camp.

Most of the time Mimi had her own counselor. One year she had two. That was the year the girl counselors cried when Katie and I picked Mimi up. She must have made quite an impression on the girls. I have a series of photos with these two lovely young high school students just bawling and hanging all over Mimi. Secretly, I loved that she had affected these young ladies so powerfully.

Each Camp CAMP ended with a dinner and parents joining their camper in a goodbye ceremony. One year, out of about one hundred campers, Mimi won the "Horsemanship Award." They had one award for each activity, like canoeing and archery, so I was stunned. The director of the horseback riding activity told the audience how everyone could tell Mimi loved her time riding so much — she was nonverbal, mind you — that they gave her extra time. I loved their mission. To me, the camp was a magical place. Their staff was exceptional.

Eventually, I found out there was a camp in the works ninety miles away from home. It was being built from the ground up specifically for those with special needs. I paid attention. I joined their guild so I would get their newsletter and noted their progress. Eventually, Mimi switched to this camp, called Camp for All. Dr. Zeller, the neurologist who had diagnosed Mimi's cerebral palsy all those years ago, was one of the people behind the camp. The camp had wide, beautiful sidewalks and real air-conditioning in the cabins and the dining hall. Everything was easily wheelchair accessible. I hated giving up Camp CAMP, but the long drive was grueling.

—

Camp for All is located near Brenham, Texas. Each week of the summer, a different organization that supports children with special needs or special circumstances rents the camp for five days. Mimi went with The Arc of Greater Houston, an organization we were already familiar with.

Now, five days was not a lot of time for a family to go far, but we did our best. One year about ten years ago, Katie and I dropped Mimi off at camp and then flew to New York City. We blazed a trail up and down that city in just a few days. We managed to see Ellis Island, Central Park, and a Broadway play, did lots of window shopping, strolled through that big museum at the edge of Central Park, and so much more. I believe we wore out a pair of tennis shoes each.

One year, Rick and Katie were both working all week, so Ricky and I took a road trip after dropping Mimi off at Camp for All. I drove hundreds of miles during that five days. I still remember the songs we sang along to on the radio: "If I Had a Million Dollars" by Barenaked Ladies, and "Fly" by Sugar Ray. They were the hit songs that year, and every time I hear them now, I go back in time to our Ricky-Mom road trip.

That road trip started in San Antonio on the River Walk. I remember Ricky feeding the pigeons French fries after dinner. Then we drove to Galveston. After dinner, Ricky fed the seagulls his French fries. We played cards before bedtime. I taught him how to play gin rummy. No late nights wandering the streets for a mom and her young son. Then, we drove back northeast of San Antonio to camp to pick Mimi up at the end of her camp week. I love the open road.

During two of Mimi's summer camp years, I was able to take my elderly mother on a fun trip to Fredericksburg. We stayed in a B&B and ate out, walked, and shopped on their lovely main street. It wasn't the wild and crazy trip to New York City with Katie. More like slow-motion fun with my mom, but fun just the same. Just as Mimi was doing at camp, my mom and I made memories that will last a lifetime.

Mimi's experience at Camp for All was always great when she was assigned the right counselor. She needed someone with the heart of a mother. The only exceptions were the first two years, when tenacity was the perfect quality for Mimi's buddy. Her buddy was a young lady studying sports therapy in college. This lady actually got Mimi in the pool every day, and I have photos to prove it. Mimi despised being in a pool and went ballistic with any splashing. It was her tactile defensiveness kicking in. Mimi loved the idea of getting in the pool, but if the water wasn't completely still, she freaked.

I knew Mimi wasn't the easiest camper a buddy could have gotten. As a mother, I knew all the tricks and wrote detailed notes about getting her to eat or to lay her head down to sleep. For me, she would do anything. It was why I always brought back a gift for the counselor to let them know how much I appreciated them.

When Mimi was thirty, I decided it was time to let summer camp go. That first year, when July rolled around, I feared Mimi would ask me to "pack." She did not. Maybe she also knew camp was to be left in the past.

I vowed to fill her life with new activities. For over twenty years, summer camp had been her very own vacation.

A bunch of years ago, I had some of my favorite Mimi summer camp photos enlarged to 11" × 14" and framed. They hang in the hallway that leads to Mimi's room. We have dubbed it "Mimi's Adventure Wall." I placed the photo of her perched atop a horse as the first photo at the entrance of the hallway, so Mimi would always see it first. The horse's mane is beautifully braided. Mimi is wearing a white helmet. There are also photos of her in a canoe, fishing, hanging out next to a donkey, and swinging on the ropes course.

—

In 2011, I wrote a column in *The Tribune* about one of Mimi's summer camp experiences that left me befuddled.

The Tribune
You Gotta Laugh — "Zip Lines and Boas"
Written by Dixie Frantz
Published August 17, 2011

Our special needs daughter asks me at least once a day to take her for a little stroll around the block. It has probably been the first of June since our last walk because of the heat. Although I don't hit any of the notes nearly as well as Mr. Rogers, I have been known to start out singing a couple of bars of "It's a Beautiful Day in the Neighborhood" as I roll Mimi's wheelchair down our driveway.

Unfortunately, Mimi doesn't understand words like drought, parched, crispy or 103 degrees in the shade. And yep, at the rate this summer has been going, it could be late October before we make it even once around the block. I don't know about you, but I think this heat is gettin' to me.

It is probably why this year, in particular, I was a tad conflicted packing up Mimi's stuff for camp. Each last week of July, one of the hottest weeks of the camp season, Mimi heads off for five days of horseback riding, fishing, canoeing, archery, petting reptiles and furry creatures, tea parties, carnivals and zip lines. Did I mention there is also a heated pool?

Now if you would think a pool would be the perfect place to cool down ... you would be correct. Except, of course, Mimi hates large bodies of water. I think it is the splashing she detests, but I am not certain. Explain to me how an almost non-verbal young lady can talk a couple of counselors out of even dipping her piggies in the cool H2O? Obviously, she has had years of practice in counselor manipulation.

I remember when our youngest used to help me drop Mimi off at camp.

"Gosh mom, this place is so fun. Can I spend the week here?" Ricky said when he was about eight or nine after getting a glimpse of the camp's zip line course.

To this day, Ricky has been in love with very high places.

Yep, in my humble opinion the special needs camp is as close as you can get to camping paradise ... thankfully with lots of blessed air conditioning.

But the whole time Mimi was at camp, all I could think about was how blazin' hot it was. If my deodorant was on the verge of failing me while I hung out in Fredericksburg, I thought, Mimi must surely be melting in a little puddle on her horse saddle. And then I'd think about how she was now 27 and maybe she was getting too old for camp. This just might have to be her last year. I thought those thoughts all of the five days Mimi was at camp, but especially on the long drive to pick her up as I struggled to keep my speedometer from exceeding the speed limit. Was I just experiencing a severe case of "Mom guilt," or was it the sizzling heat? I didn't have a clue.

And then finally, the five days were up. My car rolled into the dusty camp parking lot on Friday morning thirty minutes before the official pick-up time. As I entered the dimly lit dining hall, I looked all around for Mimi. A huge group of campers and counselors were singing near the stage and performing hand gestures to some song I couldn't make out. My ears refused to work. My mission was to find Mimi ... and fast. It was a few anxious minutes, but I finally spotted her in the middle of the crowd of campers/counselors laughing it up. After I'd gotten a tearful hug in, my tears, not her tears, Miss Cynthia grabbed me and pulled me over to a table covered with lots of photographs.

"Mimi had her BEST CAMP EVER," Cynthia declared loudly above the singing hoard.

Cynthia is the awesome lady that helps run the whole shebang. She always handpicks a "buddy" for Mimi. My guess was this year Miss Amanda must have been the perfect choice. Amanda is a young special education teacher that I had met when I dropped Mimi off. I noticed that she oozed confidence, but hey, it was her first year at camp. Cynthia showed me lots of pictures of Mimi on the stage dancing and laughing. By the time I had driven home, there were emailed photographs of Mimi petting a boa constrictor, wearing a feather boa at a tea party, riding the zip line and a couple with Mimi on a horse. Every photo containing my camper included a beaming smile.

Perhaps Miss Cynthia will never know how close I came to letting the toastiest summer on record be Mimi's last camp adventure. Was it divine intervention that caused her to grab me by the arm? I think so. Mr. Rogers was right. It is a beautiful day in the neighborhood.

—

One of the programs Mimi loved attending during the school year was Saturday Fun Day. It was six hours on a Saturday once or twice a month with The Arc of Greater Houston. There were between five and eight individuals with special needs who normally attended. Mimi loved this wonderful respite program. Miss Cynthia was the lovely lead person who came out with her merry band of volunteers. The Village Learning Center allowed the Arc to use their bus to transport everyone to their destination. Mimi was able to do things with the group like attend plays, movies, and various area festivals, go bowling, visit crafting events, and always lunch out.

I think lunch was everyone's favorite part of the event. Luby's was often voted as their favorite destination. Everyone knew Mimi's favorite lunch was the plate with a piece of fried chicken, mashed potatoes, gravy, and a vegetable. The easiest way for Mimi to plow through that plate was for someone to cut the chicken off the bone into bite-sized pieces and mix everything into the mashed potatoes. Miss Cynthia said it was a beautiful thing to watch her devour everything on her plate. Since the girl was a messy eater, I tried to remember to put a kitchen towel for her lap in her backpack to catch the food spillage. When I picked her up and lifted her into my car, I noticed all the leftover veggies and chunks of mashed potatoes that had accumulated in the sides of her wheelchair. It was a mess, yet a beautiful thing to behold.

Chapter Eleven
The Stars Align in High School

Don't let what you cannot do interfere
with what you can do.

– John Wooden

Mimi's high school years were just wonderful. Mimi had great teachers, even though she didn't make any great breakthroughs physically, mentally, or emotionally. Teachers even lightened up on the hugging rule. They realized it was an integral part of her personality and an important way she expressed herself. Mimi was a little social animal and had many great opportunities to participate in high school life despite her limited abilities.

For instance, homecoming is a huge thing in the South. Katie and Ricky both participated in high school football games and went to all the dances. I still have remnants of a couple of their homecoming mums and boutonnieres in a drawer somewhere, collecting dust bunnies.

Mimi never attended a homecoming dance or the big football games. Wheelchairs don't work very well in a high school stadium. Mimi and I did attend a couple of football games at ground level where her sister Katie pumped her pom-poms and Ricky played high school football. I think Mimi enjoyed the cheerleaders more than what was happening on the field.

One year, something wonderful happened during homecoming while Mimi was at the ninth-grade high school campus. There was someone at the high school who wanted to make mums for all the girls and boutonnieres for the boys in the life skills and applied skills classes. It was so lovely to have Mimi and her friends included in a timeless high school tradition. Although Mimi did not understand all the pomp and circumstance around the homecoming tradition, she loved all the excitement. And that mum she wore was pretty darn special.

—

In 2002, I wrote a column for *The Observer* about homecoming mums that came from an unexpected place.

The Observer
You Gotta Laugh —
"Mums, Dance Dates Herald Fall Homecomings"
Written by Dixie Frantz
Published September 18, 2002

"Son, ya gotta date yet for Homecoming? You know time is running awfully short," I said in my most encouraging and supportive voice to Ricky, my pokey sophomore in high school. This mom has been poised on the starting block to sprint toward the local floral establishment ever since the Homecoming mum display went up weeks ago. Ordering things is my specialty.

Come to think of it, these haunting dreams also started right about the time I began gently prodding Ricky about the dance. Somewhere between R.E.M. and R.O.M. sleep, I'm all alone in a dark craft store loading up my cart with dozens of white silk mums, miles of ribbon and streamers, plastic footballs and megaphones, glitter, cow bells, beads, and plastic bags full of hot glue sticks ... all for the purpose of makin' that perfect Homecoming mum for Ricky's big date. Then I get to the checkout stand and mysteriously my debit card is declined. Aw nuts! Next comes screaming and I wake up in a cold sweat. Actually, there is absolutely no possible happy ending to that dream. I'm not the least bit crafty. Flunked Popsicle stick construction in the second grade.

Personally, I think my son, like lots of young hulksters out there, are scared to ask an itty-bitty girl to a dance. Wimps. Let's face it. When it comes to females, most dudes his age are pretty much gutless relying on third and fourth parties to arrange the date. Indicating there were three prospects on his list, he said, "I'm workin' on it, mom."

I'm hoping my friendly parental nudge has everything to do with advancing Ricky's social skills rather than the allure of the Homecoming mum. But ya gotta admit those mums are pretty cool.

Our college kiddo had her vast collection of high school mums hanging on the back of her closet door for years. Katie finally packed them away in her cedar chest and carted them off to her first apartment last month along with all her worldly possessions. I was sad to see Katie ... and her mums go. Gonna miss my girl ... and all the simple things like that wonderful swishing sound the ribbons and streamers made when the closet door shut.

My absolute favorite Homecoming mum holds an almost spiritual quality. Mimi, our handicapped lass, got one last year in a most unconventional way when she hit her first year of high school.

You may not know it, but there are countless angels floating every day down the halls of our schools performing all manner of kindnesses. Sure, they rarely make the 6:00 news, but they are out there. It is why I thought you ought to know about one in particular.

You can imagine my surprise when last year I walked down the driveway to de-plane Mimi from the handicapped bus. The girl was wearing this amazing Homecoming mum on her shirt. I asked the bus driver if she knew who gave it to her. "Nope," was her answer. All I could get out of Mimi was, "Wow," as she proudly tugged on the ribbons and streamers.

Geez, by the looks of the mum I mentally noted that somebody had sure put some thought into its making. The ribbons and streamers were much shorter than normal. The perfect length for a girl in a wheelchair, otherwise they would have gotten caught in the spokes. And it even had her name in silver glitter along one of the ribbons. Did I mention there was also all manner of beads, bells, megaphones, and plastic footballs?

It was not until the following week that I was able to get Mary, one of the classroom aides, to spill her guts. Seems there is a certain secretary to one of the assistant principals at the high school that takes orders from students to make up mums every year. Friday morning of the big Homecoming game, the secretary asked if she could store some mums in the closet of the special ed room. That was all she said. It wasn't until later that day the special education teachers, who were the only ones "in" on the surprise, took out the mums and passed them around to all the special needs students in their class. The secretary had gifted each special needs student with one of her homemade mums or a garter. Mary told me it sure was something watching our special kids go down the hall just like the rest of the student body with their Homecoming mums and garters.

I am not certain if Sydney realizes this since she's probably the type of lady that does nice things all the time for people. But she did an exceptionally nice thing for a bunch of special kids. And she also made this mom cry.

Now if I can just find an angel flying around out there that can get my son a date. Being ever the eternal optimist, I have about decided if Ricky doesn't make it to Homecoming ... there's always the Valentine's Dance in the spring. Those wimpy Valentine corsages may not be a humongo Homecoming mum, but at least it is a step in the right direction.

—

I never thought in my wildest dreams that Mimi would be capable of attending her high school prom. Not in a million years. Mimi was an extremely social and delightful young lady, but mentally not the right age for such an event.

Mimi had great teachers who one day floated the idea to parents that it was about time for the life skills class to attend their prom. Before that year, it had never happened. I liken it to the perfect storm. Great teachers and parents willing to give their kids the chance to step out in a huge way! When parents and teachers started talking about the possibility of our students attending prom, we weren't sure it was going to happen. There were challenges.

First, it was a high school rule that only the teachers and aides were allowed to chaperone, under any circumstances. Yep, that meant no parents allowed. Also, the venue was all the way in Houston, about forty-five minutes away, at a downtown hotel. After a few parent-teacher meetings, a plan was hatched. Parents agreed to split the cost of a limo for the students to ride with the teachers and aides.

The boys in the class also would participate in a CBI, or "community-based instruction," for the rental of tuxes. The young ladies were to arrange for their own attire. Mimi wore a light purple sleeveless long dress with a wrist corsage purchased by her parents.

But Mimi did present a unique challenge. She was the only who used a wheelchair. Katie and I decided that was not going to stop us. We rented a hotel room at the venue, had help to physically get Mimi into the limo, and loaded up her wheelchair in my car. It helped that the other students who were riding in the limo, and their parents, came to our house first. Lots of photographs were taken before everyone left our driveway for the big event.

I was amazed when several weeks later I received a photo taken of Mimi at her high school prom. Someone had actually lifted Mimi from the wheelchair and placed her on a chair. She looked just like a princess.

—

In 2006, I wrote a column for *The Observer* about a very special prom.

The Observer
You Gotta Laugh —
"Teachers Make Prom Happen for Special Seniors"
Written by Dixie Frantz
Published April 26, 2006

I never went to my high school prom. How many of us can say that? Betcha quite a few if we took a hand count right now. C'mon, don't be shy. You know who you are.

Suppose there were several reasons why I didn't go. The family moved to Texas from Colorado in the middle of my senior year. Dad's company transferred him yet again. The biggie for me was probably my very small circle of best school buds. It was painfully about as wide as the circumference of a number two pencil.

Do I have any regrets? Maybe a couple, but not so much. I have been most fortunate to have participated in the whole prom mystique through the kids. I've sat in many a beauty parlor while Katie was getting her prom "up do" constructed. Gotta tell ya, if you live for drama, betcha nine dollars the local hair salon is THE place to be on prom day. According to Linda, one of the hairdressers where I hang once a month, most of the girls are SO VERY NICE, but she has seen her share of "Promzillas."

I have also been there to hold Ricky's large hand during his date's corsage order. I was the one that suggested the blinking lights accessory. And with each child, I've gotten unique perspectives.

The oldest was my party animal. Katie went to FOUR proms, beginning with her sophomore year. By the time senior year tornadoed in, she was dating a young man from another high school and ended up going to two proms that year. Thank the powers that be, they were on different Saturdays, or surely Katie would have figured out a way to make appearances at both.

Ricky went to prom last year and, I feel certain, it would have not happened at all without lots of prodding with a stick from his mom. A social butterfly where girls were concerned, he was not in high school. Having two sisters you would have thought girls would not have been this huge mystery. But they were to him. It is why I started working on Ricky when he was a high school freshman. My goals were tiny baby steps. Just ask a girl to a dance for Pete's sake. Think Ricky finally made it to his first dance, homecoming, when he was a junior. I can safely say that my college freshman is now totally up to grade level in the social skills arena.

Always thought my special needs child would, like her mom, never attend her prom. That was especially the case upon learning parents were not allowed, under any circumstances, to chaperone the dance. I can certainly see why they have the rule. What student in their right, or left mind, would want one of their parents present at their prom? That's just plain yuck, if you ask me.

But there was still this hard spot in the left side of my heart, like a stone, that would make me tear up if I thought about it too much. Geez, wasn't it enough that Mimi had been so very different from the rest of the student body her entire life? Couldn't she, for just one night, be a small part of a normal high school milestone?

All that changed a couple of years ago. The special education teachers at Mimi's high school picked up the ball and scored a three-pointer in my book. I watched from afar and silently hoped it would turn into a tradition and not just a one-time event.

The teachers, and even some of the classroom aides, volunteered to chaperone the graduating senior special needs students that year. Not only that ... they organized stuff like arranging for the limo. They made ordering tuxes and shopping for dresses into a learning experience during a field trip. They had prom planning meetings with the parents and students after school. I was deeply impressed. Organizing prom for my own kids was a lot like building a skyscraper with Legos ... one teeny block at a time. I couldn't even imagine what they went through.

It is the reason this past Saturday night, Mimi attended her own high prom with classmates Kelsie, and six very handsome young lads decked out in their spiffy tuxes. Mimi's teacher also came to our house early, and fixed Mimi's hair, as she had so many times during school. You should see Miss Jeannette French braid hair with your own eyeballs. The lady has magic fingers. The students all rode in a limo with their teachers that left from our house. My daughter Katie and I followed in the family truckster with Mimi's wheelchair. The high school prom was held in the Hyatt Hotel ballroom downtown.

Mimi didn't last too long before getting all tuckered out, which was totally expected. Night owl she is not. It was why I had rented a room at the hotel, and we three girls had our own after-prom slumber party.

So, these things I know to be certain. I may have not attended my high school prom, but because of some very wonderful special education teachers, Mimi will always be able to say, she partied with the rest of the graduating class of 2006!

—

When Mimi neared the end of high school, I saw the writing on the wall. I saw it much earlier than Rick, but there was no convincing him. We did not have the conversation about adding "the label" very often. We could not. Mimi would always be a delightful two-year-old from an intellectual perspective. What do we do with that? We were fine with who she was. It had become apparent the world was not — and would punish her for it.

During transition planning from high school, the professionals around the table at the ARD meetings give you information. Most of the time these nuggets do not compute for the parents. Parents with a special needs child are always trying to stay ahead of the next crisis or challenge. But what I finally ingested into my brain was that there were state programs that helped subsidize, and sometimes pay for, things like respite, a day program, and dental expenses. Depending on the disability, there might be other things they might pay for. As I finally took my head out of the sand, I dove headfirst into the deep end of the pool. I learned what these programs might look like for Mimi. I realized high school was the time to have the "mentally retarded" label applied. It was now or never.

I had a meeting with Mimi's high school diagnostician. She had come to know our daughter over several years. This lady was the diagnostician who clearly treated her job as a vocation. She let me know the difficulty in testing Mimi, but she had a plan. She apparently had been thinking about it a lot. She decided to take portions of two tests to come up with an IQ number.

Weeks later, I read her testing report and cried. The results were spot on. Her report was sprinkled generously with kindness, compassion, and accuracy. Mimi was now labeled "moderately mentally retarded." The powers that be in the state of Texas would be okay with her findings. And Rick — he came around, reluctantly. Again, I believe it was divine intervention that Mimi had this particular high school diagnostician. I will be forever grateful for her gentleness, wisdom, and grace.

Just like teachers and therapists, there are great diagnosticians. I never thought of labels with regards to Mimi. She was unique. It was a sad reality the day Mimi had to be labeled with intellectual challenges. I was thankful the diagnostician helped put that reality behind us. And the upside: Mimi would be eligible for state-sponsored programs.

—

The year Mimi aged out of public school was 2006, when she turned twenty-two. There were over nine hundred students in her graduating class at Kingwood High School. I had been to several high school graduations, and they were nuts. Just parking in Houston's NRG Stadium and walking to the venue, where the Houston Texans played football, required nerves and buns of titanium. There would be hours of sitting and other logistics to consider, like the climb with Mimi, which would not be worth the view. On some level, our family would have loved seeing her being pushed across the stage, waving to the crowd, and hugging everyone. But the hours to make that happen would have been so grueling for Mimi. I felt certain Mimi would not have enjoyed that part of the program.

We opted for the more intimate graduation ceremony that was offered at the high school. The venue was a stage where school plays were performed. A handful of students with special needs would be graduating. Parents and family in the audience were treated to a slide show of their graduating seniors. It was interesting watching Mimi sit on the stage with her graduating peers. She sat so quietly in her wheelchair, with one hand resting on her chin. She looked like a china doll in her flowing baby-blue graduation gown. It swallowed her petite little body. The caps were all too large for her small head, so she went without one.

There was a reception in her class afterward, with cookies and punch. It was the perfect graduation event, tailor-made with Mimi and the other students in mind.

—

In 2006, I wrote a column for *The Observer* about riding roller coasters and Mimi's high school graduation.

The Observer
You Gotta Laugh —
"Riding the Roller Coaster Toward Graduation"
Written by Dixie Frantz
Published May 31, 2006

Last week was an emotional week. If you happen to have in your pos-session a child that just graduated from high school, you are a member of the exclusive club. It felt like riding that creaky wooden coaster they tore down recently at the dearly departed Astroworld amusement park. You are delirious about your child's accomplishments one minute, and then, don't want school to end the next. Yep, life is a lot like the two-minute rickety coaster that started out kinda on the slow side, crept up a steep hill, and paused ever so slightly at the top. Then there was the wild, high-speed ride to the very bottom and twists and turns and, well, you remember the rest. The scariest part for me was the dark tunnel. Excuse me while I unbuckle my imaginary seat belt, attempt to stand, and retrieve my purse from the rollercoaster attendant.

Rollercoasters remind me of the many ups and downs of life. I'm almost recovered, but not fully. You see, my very last child graduated last week. For the past twenty-one wonderful, and sometimes terrifying years, I've had at least one of my three babes in a neighborhood school.

And now that era of my life, and theirs, is over forever. Just like the day Astroworld closed it gates, there will be no more hair-raising rides on the Texas Cyclone.

Seems just yesterday the special bus lumbered down our street belching diesel to pick Mimi up for her first day of Early Childhood at a local elementary school. Way back during the days of the horse-drawn school bus, no seriously, it WAS that long ago though, they let the drivers honk their horns to let moms know they were waiting out front. That first day was the absolute worst. Reminds me of that first huge drop to the very bottom of the coaster ride. Mimi was just three years old when a stranger in a miniature yellow bus drove up to take her to school. I musta cried a jumbo box of Kleenex tissues right there on the curb. And that was all before the driver rounded our cul-de-sac.

Last week, Mimi and I said goodbye to Miss Jessie and Mr. Roy. They were the awesome driver and aide that picked Mimi up the entire last year of high school. Heck, we've had a large treasure chest of silver and gold bus drivers over the years. I'll never forget their cheerfulness and perkiness that early in the morning. And betcha nine dollars, they will always remember my severely rumpled appearance. Hey, I was allowed. It was 6:30 in the a.m. ... and I'd just gotten off the coaster.

The school held a special graduation celebration at the high school for Mimi and nine of her fellow graduates last week. Mimi had the option of attending the mega-graduation ceremony with about 900 of her closest friends, but we decided to pass.

There were many special moments during that final graduation event. One of the students gave a most eloquent appreciation speech. I remember Chance mentioned that his teachers talked him into taking a speech class. He indicated that he hated that class, and tried to quit several times, except for the persistence of his teachers. Chance thanked them for their encouragement. How fitting that Chance should deliver the speech.

Chance had also been one of Mimi's classmates so many years before in Early Childhood. He now works as a cashier at the local grocery store and has checked my overflowing cart out more times than I can count on fingers and toes. Miss Courtney predicted that someday Chance would manage his own store.

The reason I remember him so vividly is because I have his handprints on a quilt hanging on Mimi's wall. I did the sewing and purchased it during an elementary school fundraiser. The entire class and teachers had both their handprints in blue paint on one of the many quilt blocks. But Chance's block was the most unusual. Because he couldn't physically open one of his hands, just one was painted and printed twice side-by-side on the quilt block.

After his speech we all wildly clapped. Then Miss Courtney stepped up to the podium and said a bunch of really nice things about the ten students seated on the stage. Each graduate smiled shyly as some of their awesome attributes were read to the audience. Mimi looked surprised sitting up on the stage in her wheelchair when her own name was read. I had a sneaky feeling her great bear hugs would be mentioned. I wasn't disappointed.

The ceremony closed with a slide show presentation of the last school year complete with dances, school parties, prom, field day, and then the tearjerker moment. A baby picture of each student slowly flashed across the screen, and finally, their graduation photo. I would have been surprised if there was a dry eye in the house. Thanks to Miss Courtney who warned me to bring lots of tissues.

"Geez, Mimi's graduation was way more fun than mine last year," said our son Ricky afterward.

"No, yours was lots of fun also. This was just different," I said, wiping a tear and a streak of black mascara running down the corner of my right eye.

The Frantz family may have witnessed the end of an era, but heck, there are lots more roller coasters out there to ride. See ya at the amusement park of life!

—

The friendships I made with mothers of special needs children led us to discussions, many years before graduation, about what happens after high school. We knew exactly what it meant. Nearly all our special children would not go to college. Most would not be able to hold down a job or drive a car. So, what exactly happens? Those with intellectual disabilities do not just fall into a black hole and disappear. The days of institutions are pretty much long gone, thank you, Jesus. Institutions still exist in the state of Texas, and are the most expensive and least humane way for those with special needs to live out their days.

Most adults with intellectual disabilities come home after graduation and hang out ALL DAY with their mothers, or other family members, FOREVER.

Chapter Twelve
Life at The Village

I can't change the direction of the wind,
but I can adjust my sails to always reach my destination.

—Jimmy Dean

Located in Kingwood, Texas, The Village Learning Center, or simply "The Village" to most of us, was created in 2000 by two lovely mothers. Kim and Linda's mission was to create opportunities for adults with intellectual disabilities to thrive in their own neighborhoods. It started out slowly, with a day center for just a few Villagers in a small shopping center space. A few years later, the Village acquired a government grant to rehab an old daycare center. This greatly increased the number of Villagers who were able to attend. Today, they service well over a hundred Villagers through their quality day program.

Eventually they added a thrift store, a residential facility called Stoney Glen for adults with IDD (which stands for "intellectual and developmental disabilities") that also included a couple of respite beds, accessible transportation, and HUD ("housing and urban development") apartments for those with intellectual disabilities. That is just the short list.

Mimi started going to the after-school program at what she called the "center" — The Village mentioned above — while I worked with Rick in his business. The school bus dropped her off at the day center after high school.

I picked her up in the late afternoon. Eventually, the program expanded, and when Mimi aged out of school, she transitioned to their day program five days a week.

Mimi attended the Village day center program for twelve years. Once a week, her class went bowling. It was her favorite day of the week! A wheelchair-accessible bus picked Mimi up from our driveway Monday through Friday. Mimi would have gone to the Village seven days a week if it were open. She loved the place that much! The day center gave her social opportunities to mingle with friends and staff. But the Village was so much more. Mimi continued to learn, grow intellectually, and learn new words. The staff continued to challenge her to participate in activities when she would have rather just sat back and observed from the sidelines.

When Rick and I finally took ownership of Mimi's handicap-accessible van, I started picking her up from the Village in the afternoons. As I waded through the room to grab Mimi, there were lots of the other Villagers waiting for their ride each day. PJ immediately comes to mind. He called me "Mimi's mom." It is a label I will lovingly treasure the rest of my life.

Mimi was a social animal. It was one of her greatest gifts. She nurtured relationships like charms on a bracelet, with few words, a toothy smile, and a huge hug.

In 2011, my friend Mary and I started and facilitated a group of Village parents in order to keep communication lines open with the day center on behalf of our special needs adults. The Village's VIP (stands for "very important parents") group was born several years after the day center moved to its current location.

Now, I will be the first to admit, I am NOT a leader-type person. My comfort zone is more behind the scenes. But Mary and I felt so strongly about the value of communication between parents and the Village that we just stepped up. The difficulty remained that many of the Villagers who attended the day program could not tell their parents or guardians what they did all day. Our intention was to be a partner with the Village. I facilitated the parent group.

For nearly ten years, we forged and nurtured friendships, supported each other, shared information, put on dances for our Village adults, provided volunteers for Village fundraisers, invited Village staff to our meetings, and so much more. I eventually wrote an article for the Village newsletter each month. When Mimi left us, I had to step away.

—

For several years, the Village has held a talent show fundraiser. The event features community talent in two categories: special needs and everyone else. Talents such as magic, comedy, singing, and dancing were showcased in both categories. What an absolutely fun and unique night!

Of course, my husband's favorite part of the event was the silent cake auction. His sweet tooth is legendary! One year, Rick bid on two large cakes. It is a super fun event that continues to surprise and enchant each year.

A couple of years ago, Dr. Penn, our local pediatrician/magician, participated in the talent show. He performed his magic act for the crowd. Mimi and I attended the event. It was so nice to see him again. Mimi was probably about thirty years old by then. There were huge hugs all around as he noticed us at a nearby table. Imagine our surprise when he got on stage and dedicated his magic act to Mimi. There were gasps in the audience, as most everyone in the room knew our Mimi. It was a magical moment for this mom.

—

The Village was instrumental in providing parents with something called "respite." Now, respite is an interesting word. Parents and caregivers of those with a disability intimately know the meaning. It is especially important when the disability requires that you can't leave your loved one alone for even one second. Basically, respite is short-term, or temporary, care of the sick or disabled for a few hours or days, designed to provide relief to the regular caregiver.

When Katie and Ricky were still home before heading off to college, I could run an errand, like going to the cleaners or the grocery store, and know that Mimi was in good hands. Mimi could never be left at home alone. Never. Ever.

The challenge started when the kids left for college. Imagine if you do not have a way for both parents to attend your college child's parents' weekend, college football game, or even graduation because you don't have someone to watch your disabled adult child. It also means going on a date with your husband is challenging. Rick and I tended to tag team each other when there were night meetings. Rick would attend a meeting at night, and I would stay home with Mimi, and vice versa.

Of course, I had respite during the day when Mimi was at the Village day center. It afforded me time for my hair emergencies (what I call my monthly hair appointments), volunteering, dental and doctor visits, and household errands.

After the Village day center opened, a home was created for adults with intellectual disabilities. In total there are maybe fifteen or sixteen IDD residents who call Stoney Glen their home, and they have lots of supervision. The residents also attend the Village day center during the week. A few beds at Stoney Glen were reserved for respite.

In the beginning, Rick and I used Stoney Glen for respite for several hours at a time. We started taking Mimi there when Rick and I had a grown-up meeting to attend together. It started out slowly, with a few hours here and there. Finally, we were brave enough to try an overnight stay. Sometime later a whole weekend happened. Eventually, I was comfortable participating in occasional events at Katie's and Ricky's colleges. Each time Mimi stayed, I talked with the staff about how everything went at Stoney Glen. We eventually worked up to a week away for an adventure. Respite wasn't cheap, but it was necessary, and Mimi loved being at Stoney Glen! She called it the "house."

In 2008, we decided to go on an adventure every two years. Actually, I probably needed it more than Rick. I was tired of living through all my friends' trip photos on Facebook. Wanderlust could have been my middle name, especially after the trip to Italy Katie and I took in 2000. I wanted to share some of those magical moments with Rick. That was the year Rick and I went to Rome. Ricky was finishing up his summer abroad program in Spain and met us a few days into the trip. We climbed to the top of St. Peter's rotunda, threw coins in a famous fountain, and marveled at the Pantheon and Colosseum. Mimi was twenty-four years old and more than ready to get her parents out of her hair for a few days. We were gone for six glorious days and ate lots of gelato.

In 2010, we traveled to Florence, Verona, Venice, and to visit the artist who had carved the crucifix at our home parish, St. Martha. Florence became our most favorite city, with its abundant art museums and magical churches. We were in serious love with Italy and again ate way too much gelato.

In 2012, for our fortieth wedding anniversary, Rick and I went to Paris, where we attended Mass at Notre Dame cathedral and strolled near the Eiffel Tower. We toured Rodin's museum and saw where Napoleon was buried. His showy tomb was way over the top for Rick. Then there was the Mona Lisa at the Louvre, and yes, it is true what they say — Leonardo da Vinci's painting is very small. Several days into our trip, we met our son, Ricky, and his lovely wife, Kate, and toured the beaches of Normandy, the American cemetery, and Mont-Saint-Michel, the monastery out in the mud flats.

In 2014, we traveled to Holland and Bruges, Belgium, the city of chocolate shops and churches. Ricky and Kate met us in Holland. Part of the trip was research for a book about my mom, and part was pure adventure. Visits to the Anne Frank House, Van Gogh Museum, the cities of Delft and Haarlem, and the Kinderdijk windmills were just a few of our adventures. Eventually, we parted ways with Ricky and Kate. They went to Greece. Rick and I moved on for a few days in Bruges. Our mission was to find Michelangelo's statue with Madonna and the baby Jesus. We brought back lots of Belgian chocolate and Dutch cheese.

In 2016, Rick was diagnosed with stage 4 clear cell kidney cancer, and we stayed home. But Stoney Glen continued to be there for us in a huge way. Stoney Glen made it possible for us to get through a year of cancer treatment. I don't know how I would have made it through Rick's cancer journey without Stoney Glen!

In 2018, shortly before Mimi left us, Rick and I traveled back to Italy. We visited Florence, Venice, and Siena. Physically, Rick wasn't in the best of shape. That became evident when we got lost the second day in Florence. We walked using an app that got us so lost! Literally fifteen miles later, we made it back to our hotel. Rick was never the same for the rest of the trip. His stamina was zapped. We tried to make the best of it.

Chapter Thirteen
Making Mimi's World Flat

Do not go where the path may lead. Go instead
where there is no path and leave a trail.

– Ralph Waldo Emerson

The ADA, or the Americans with Disabilities Act of 1990, was signed on July 26, 1990, by President George H. W. Bush. Mimi was six years old, and the world was not yet flat and accessible for those in wheelchairs. The ADA was modeled after the Civil Rights Act of 1964. It protected the rights of those with disabilities regarding employment, government services, and other aspect of public life, such as access.

—

Being married to an engineer who only sees solutions, not problems, has made having a child whose mode of transportation was a wheelchair liberating. Throughout the years, all I had to do was make an innocent remark about a difficulty or challenge involving Mimi, and Rick was grabbing his engineering pad and coming up with a solution. He could not make the outside world flat, so he concentrated on our house and property.

Rick would sometimes start the conversation and ask for my input into what would make my life easier in caring for Mimi. Depending on the complexity of Mimi's needs, we might talk about a design for many weeks. That is how Mimi's accessible/guest bathroom evolved.

Except for the year we lived in Michigan, Mimi lived in the same one-story house at the end of a peaceful cul-de-sac all her life. A two-story house would have never worked for her. Over Mimi's life, our home changed many times, and we created an environment that functioned for our family, but really accommodated the many special needs of our daughter. The modifications allowed Mimi wheelchair access to pretty much the whole house and outdoors.

Before we moved into the home in 1981, Rick, the resident engineer, checked some website noting the elevation of the lot. Who does that? My guess is engineers do. It served us well. We have never flooded — knock heavily on plywood.

It is probably why we have always sheltered in place with Mimi when necessary. There was a category 3 hurricane named Rita that was a serious issue for the Houston area. In September 2005, three million Houston area residents evacuated pretty much all at the same time. No one had ever been through anything like this before.

The news reported traffic was locked up for two days. People ran out of gas and food. Their cars broke down and it was hot. A number of deaths were attributed to the evacuation. If we had gotten on the road, I feel Mimi would have perished from the gas fumes from the other vehicles and the heat, like several others did. I am not certain why we stayed and sheltered in place. Divine intervention?

Then when Hurricane Ike came Houston's way in September 2008, the Frantz family again sheltered in place. It turned out to be a great plan. We weathered the storm. Except for one thing. There would be no electricity for about two weeks for many, many residents.

We had a small generator and were able to, among other things, keep a fan circulating in Mimi's room at night. But then the temperatures started to climb. There were shortages of fuel and food. After a few days, I called Rick's sister, Mary. Mary and her husband, Larry, lived north of Austin and gladly offered us a place to stay. Rick and Katie stayed behind to keep an eye on our house with the hope services would be restored any day.

I remember sleeping in Mary and Larry's guest room with Mimi in a king-sized bed. Mimi and I would turn in around nine p.m. I'd place pillows on one side of the bed so she wouldn't fall out, and then I would crawl in beside her. Mimi was twenty-one at the time, but still a sweet little girl. But try convincing a "two-year-old" it is time to go to sleep. It went something like this:

"Mimi, lay your head down and go night night," said I.

"Night," said Mimi sweetly.

Wash, rinse, and repeat these two lines about a hundred times before Mimi finally laid her head down to sleep.

—

When Katie was in high school, we changed the footprint of our little house by adding 234 square feet on the east side. We took four small rooms located right next to each other and made them larger. The reason was to enlarge the small guest bathroom to make it an accessible bathroom that didn't also scream "handicapped." It just made sense to enlarge the three other small rooms along the east elevation.

You might ask the reason for the drastic measures? Our original small, rectangular guest bath had a narrow entry door and was the width of the bathtub and commode. If you think about most houses, the bathroom doorways are almost always narrow. That is just how they make them —

wide enough for a person to walk through. The narrow door concept makes perfect sense if everyone is ambulatory.

When Mimi was little, I would carry her into the bathroom in my arms and lay her on a thick towel in front of the tub. This got more awkward as she aged. It wasn't many years before I was carrying her from under the arms and struggling to get us both through the doorway. And when I laid her down on the towel in front of the bathtub, her head was close to hitting the toilet, which was just beyond the tub. There just wasn't room to operate. Obviously, something had to be done.

We engaged a local home builder who also performed home renovations and talked to his designer, who did some tweaking of our design concept. The rooms that were to be enlarged were the master bathroom, laundry room, Mimi's bathroom, and one of the kids' rooms. It would take six months to complete the renovations, since there were two bathrooms — our only bathrooms — involved. After the slab was built out on the east side of our house, the framing and roof were built. The demolition and rebuilding of Mimi's bathroom was next.

The experience wasn't especially fun, since we lived in the house the entire six months during construction. Five of us shared one bathroom. Katie's room was the bedroom to be enlarged. She was displaced to the home office at the front of the house. The whole family spent lots of time in Katie's room during the renovation. It was the most fun room in the house. Of course, any place Katie is, there is a party. Katie would crank up the music and all of us would dance. We soon learned during our dance marathons that Mimi loved Paul Simon. When "The Rhythm of the Saints" or "Diamonds on the Soles of Her Shoes" were played, Rick would grab Mimi and twirl her in his arms. Mimi loved it. When she said "again," who could resist? Around and around she would go! Mimi had the cutest cackle when her dad would dip her at the end of a song.

My one solace about Mimi not being physically present anymore is that she is dancing in heaven on her new and improved legs and feet. And yes — there is certainly something sparkling on the soles of her shoes.

When the house was finally finished, I was able to easily push Mimi through the doorways of both bathrooms. Mimi's bathroom was so large I was able to get her wheelchair in the room and shut the door for privacy. The sink is open underneath to accommodate pushing Mimi closer for hand washing and brushing teeth. The commode was far enough away there was no way Mimi was hitting her head when I laid her in front of the tub. There were even longer handles on the sink faucet so she would be able to one day turn on the water herself. That never happened, but we included future possibilities for Mimi in our designs.

I was happy we included enlarging the door to the master bathroom. After both bathrooms were finished, I started drying Mimi's hair in the master bathroom. She loved the big mirrors and large space. We could sing songs, linger, and chat without someone knocking on the door and needing to use the guest bath.

—

Rick and I had a vision for the front and back yards as well. I struggled getting Mimi out of the house when her bus arrived in the morning. The front threshold was not flat enough to easily maneuver the wheelchair over, and there was not a sidewalk to wheel her to the driveway.

Slowly, a vision was realized. Our sketch was taken to a local garden designer who executed the plan with perfection. Concrete ramping slightly sloped down from the front door, allowing me to maneuver the wheelchair. A new paved path was placed from the sidewalk over to the driveway. Previously, there was no way I would take Mimi out the front door even if the threshold had allowed it. The walkway straight down to the street was steep and the curb was super scary. I had nightmares about taking Mimi down that walkway. Part of the cracked driveway was replaced and the bit where the driveway met the street was nicely flattened. I no longer worried about getting her safely out the front of our house.

Many moons later, we started work on the backyard with Mimi in mind. Years before, we had a handyman make a wooden ramp for the back door, but as Mimi's wheelchairs grew wider through the years, the ramp was deemed less safe by Rick's engineering safety standards. We wanted her to be able to participate fully, and there were other obstacles that needed flattening.

Rick and I worked in several phases. The first phase involved a slight and safe decline out the back door. Instead of wood, the area was tiled, along with the patio area. The tile was not slick when it rained and worked perfectly. Later, we added an elevated wooden deck, again with a ramping system so that Mimi could access the deck area. The deck included a restful water fountain and area seating with an umbrella. Mimi was able to eat outside with the family when the weather was nice. With Rick's attention to detail, the slight drop-off from the tile to the driveway was also accommodated. He even had the door to the detached garage widened so I would be able to move Mimi easily into the garage during inclement weather.

—

Some of Rick's projects were small but mighty. Mimi had always joined us at the kitchen table for meals. We had an oval wooden table that worked for our family of five, with a slight modification. Rick took off a portion of the table that projected underneath. Without that little piece of wood, Mimi could be pulled close to the table with everyone else. This worked for many years, until our family started to expand. Katie and Ricky got married, and suddenly our kitchen table wasn't large enough.

Rick and I did some furniture shopping to see if we could find a table that would accommodate our growing family and also accommodate Mimi. We talked to several furniture people about our kitchen table issue. Everyone looked at us like we were from Jupiter. Finally, we found a furniture company to make a custom table. Rick had a simple idea for a small table with legs just a few inches taller so Mimi could sit with her family during meals. It would be placed at the head of our new rectangular table and could easily be moved if need be. They also matched the stain to our kitchen table, so the little table didn't seem out of place. It was a proud moment for us the first time Mimi pulled up to her table for a meal.

For many years, we had carpeting throughout most of our house. After getting a "pay raise" when Ricky and Katie finally graduated college, we worked on having tile installed. It made it so much easier for Mimi to wheel herself around the house.

Mimi's last two wheelchairs grew a tad wider, making it challenging to get through her bedroom door. Because of the location of her door, the only remedy was a pocket door. We were able to achieve just a few more inches in width. It made it possible to clear the hallway and not hit the sheetrock, which was scraped and worn. The contractor also installed painted beaded paneling halfway up the wall that covered the damaged sheetrock.

We made our house accessible for lots of reasons. We had most holidays, work parties, and birthdays at our house. Our house started out just like other homes — not very accessible. When Mimi was little, it didn't matter so much. After all the modifications, it was now easier for family and friends to come to us, and come they did.

Mimi and middle school teacher working on pegs.

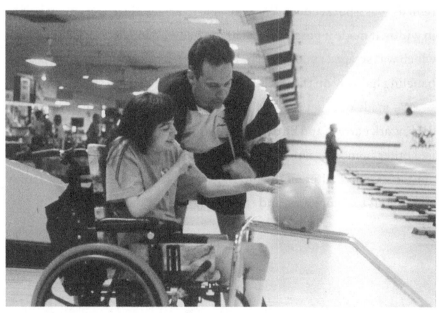

Middle school instructor and Mimi during community-based instruction bowling.

Mimi rides a horse at summer camp.

Mimi and buddies at Camp For All summer camp.

Ricky, Mimi and Katie family Christmas photo.

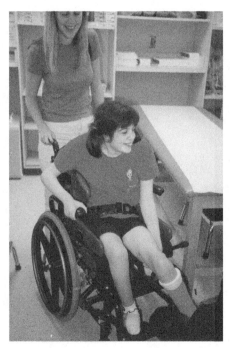

Mimi receives a pink cast after foot surgery.

Mimi gets ready for prom.

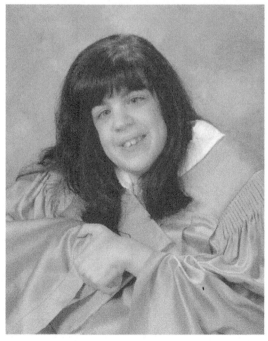

Mimi graduates from high school.

PART THREE

Chapter Fourteen

Living by the Rules

There is no education like adversity.

— Benjamin Disraeli

According to governmental entities, rules change when your disabled child turns eighteen. Your special needs child may not have aged out of public school yet, but things are going to change. Those with disabilities deal with various systems and bureaucracies that govern their lives if they want to qualify for and keep services or state and federal benefits. Doesn't that sound confusing?

One area has to do with guardianship. Applying for legal guardianship of our daughter was a weird time for us. In the grand scheme of things, it seemed ludicrous that it was something we had to do. Of course, it was obvious to us Mimi could not make decisions for herself. But clearly laws existed that would impede us from making all kinds of decisions for Mimi. I mean, she was our daughter, but only spoke a couple hundred words. Her understanding was that of a two-year-old. She couldn't sign her name. Who else was going to make decisions?

Did you know you cannot make decisions for your child after the age of eighteen if you don't have legal guardianship? Yes, and there are also a couple of different levels of guardianship. To make all decisions for Mimi, we had to have full guardianship. We also had to hire a lawyer, file legal papers, and go to court before a judge. Because we needed full guardianship, this also meant Mimi could not vote. The powers that be take this right to vote very seriously, as well they should. Be prepared to shell out a couple thousand dollars.

I had the name of an attorney who did lots of guardianships for those with special needs. She was wonderful. Rick and I hired the attorney to handle appointing us Mimi's joint guardians.

The court paid for and appointed an attorney for Mimi. The court-appointed attorney came to our house and met with Mimi and us. I recall sitting at the kitchen table with the lady, who asked Mimi some questions. Since Mimi had a limited vocabulary, there were not any responses. I recall Mimi hugged her neck twice.

When the day came for the guardianship hearing, our attorney told us Mimi did not have to come along. I kind of wished we had brought her. It might have been a bright spot for the judge, who clearly dealt with cases of family members taking care of an elderly relative more often than special needs guardianship cases. I feel certain it must have been depressing on so many levels for a judge. Mimi would have been so glad to shower her special graces on the courtroom. Rick and I were granted full, joint guardianship of Mimi after just a few minutes. Yes — we got to keep her. Every year it was our little joke — like we were going to let anyone else have her.

Every year, Rick and I were required to send to the court a three-page official and notarized document about where Mimi was living and how she was doing. There were specific questions with short answers. Every October, I sent in the document. Then, in January, I ordered the guardianship papers from the court. This certificate granted Rick and I joint full guardianship for another year. I usually asked for four or five copies. Different agencies asked us to produce them from time to time, like the day center or a government caseworker.

Someone from the court also paid a short visit each year to make sure Mimi was in good hands. Sometimes it was a surprise visit to our house or to the day center. I stopped thinking of it as an intrusion about ten years into the visits, but on some level it was annoying and one more thing we had to accommodate.

—

Then there was the first time Mimi and I walked into the MHMRA (which stands for "Mental Health Mental Retardation Authority"). They call it something different now. Mimi and I went to meet with an official who looked over the diagnostician's testing document regarding Mimi's recent new label. He quickly issued a DMR ("determination of mental retardation") form. If Mimi did not qualify as an adult with an intellectual disability, she would not receive services through the MHMRA.

The first program to which Mimi was assigned through the MHMRA as an adult was Texas Home Living. A caseworker was assigned to Mimi and assessed the services she would need to be able to live with support in our home. The program subsidized part of her day program, a little respite for her mom and dad, and some dental funds. Mimi and I met with a caseworker each month and signed paperwork. I understood their need to put their eyes on Mimi and me. There was also a lengthy yearly meeting that set services for the new year.

We appreciated the financial assistance the Texas program offered. It was certainly not enough for Mimi to live on, but I was thankful for the help. It was intrusive but bearable.

Mimi was also on a waiting list for Home Community Services, or HCS. This is also a Texas program that was designed to support families with intellectually disabled adults so they could live with their families and stay in their communities. HCS provides direct financial support to caregivers or guardians. No one could really tell me how this program would benefit Mimi. We just took it for granted HCS would be better than Texas Home Living. Many years ago, thankfully, it was decided institutions were not the answer for those with intellectual disabilities, partly because of the huge cost per person and partly because of the nature of institutions. It was determined it was so much cheaper for those with IDD to live in their communities and to place the cost of raising a disabled person on the parents and caregivers, and not so much on the state. Unfortunately, there is a long waiting list, and the monetary support is not adequate.

According to an article on Patch.com dated January 11, 2019, "Texas is among the nation's worst states when it comes to supporting people with intellectual and developmental disabilities."

The report was published by the American Network of Community Options and Resources, known as ANCOR, and United Cerebral Palsy. The report stated Texas ranked forty-ninth in the United States.

The report stated, "Texas has taken no significant steps to improve policies that help individuals with intellectual and development disabilities lead more independent and productive lives, resulting in a continued poor showing in state rankings."

Mimi's name finally came up after a thirteen-year wait. Our family was able to take advantage of this program for two years before Mimi left us.

Like Texas Home Living, HCS paid for part of her day program. HCS also paid me a foster care stipend that I used to pay for Mimi's respite, Saturday Fun Day, transportation to and from the day center, and the part of Mimi's day center that HCS did not cover. It was our decision to pick up much of the financial burden. It is what a lot of parents and caregivers naturally do.

There is cumbersome paperwork involved with the program — pages and pages of paperwork each month. Reports on having monthly fire drills, medication reports, doctor visit reports, daily activity reports, etc., were all part of the rules. A caseworker was assigned to Mimi, and it was pretty much the same drill as the other state programs. Meetings with caseworkers each month and long annual meetings.

—

Every year or so, Rick and I would wrestle with a question that was always the elephant sitting on our chests. I was reminded by a conversation with a stranger that the question is a frequent one. I will never forget the conversation I had with a contractor who was replacing our back door. When he learned our daughter had special needs, he immediately spilled his guts. He had a ten-year-old son with autism. He was already wondering what was going to happen should he die. He was divorced from his wife and had custody of his three children. He looked so worried, and his special child was so little! I don't think I had those thoughts when Mimi was that young. I just knew I would be around forever.

Rick and I would talk about this very question every few years, beginning when Katie and Ricky left the nest. It was always difficult to think about where in the world Mimi fit except in our home with her two parents to care for her. We also always agreed that a perfect scenario would be for the three of us to die on the same day — of natural causes of course. You think I am kidding?

We finally agreed the best possible housing option when both Rick and I were gone would be for Mimi to live in a small group home and have Katie check in often. Mimi's big sister would be appointed her guardian and be able to make medical and financial decisions.

We were not confident any program offered by the state of Texas would provide a place that was appropriate for Mimi to live after we died. In the few short years Mimi had been an adult, MHMRA programs had changed or gone away, and waiting lists had gotten out of control. Clearly, the disabled are not a big voting bloc that politicians make a priority.

While there are still a few institutions in the state of Texas, that option was never, ever something for Mimi. There were communities, like The Brookwood Community in Brookshire, Texas, for those with IDD. But Mimi needed to be able to take care of her physical needs to qualify. We even thought of establishing a small group home nearby with a couple of girls we knew, but that never happened for lots of reasons.

Some adults with disabilities live in assisted-living facilities and nursing homes. There are no easy answers to where in the world our adult IDD children belong after their parents can no longer care for them. I believe the disabled should be able to live safely, with dignity and respect, and to their full potential.

———

When I wasn't meeting with caseworkers or filling out reams of required paperwork, there was an important wheelchair project that would creep up, covered, figuratively speaking, in red tape. Obviously, there never was a time when I sat on the couch all day and ate bonbons.

Let me begin by saying that just maintaining a wheelchair that was required to be kept for five years was a challenge. It might have been easier if I was always in complete control of Mimi's wheelchair. But that was not possible. Mimi went to school or a day center. Sometimes staff pushed her through tight doorways, messing up the brakes on her wheelchair. Mimi pushed herself through areas that were tight. Our own house had a couple of areas that had pinch points. Mimi was famous for moving herself from her bedroom down the hallway and scraping the sheetrock walls. Wear and tear on a wheelchair are brutal.

Rick oversaw general wheelchair maintenance, like tightening brake screws. These were specially made and not replaceable from a hardware store. We learned to stockpile arm cushions. Rick replaced these a couple times a year. Did I mention it was so nice to have a hubby who was handy? Mimi sat on a special air cushion that also had to be maintained. There were occasional leaks that had to be patched, and several times it had to be sent off across the country to be professionally repaired. I finally purchased a duplicate cushion — they run about seven hundred dollars a pop.

Every five years, Medicaid allows a disabled nonambulatory person to acquire a new wheelchair. But getting that very important piece of equipment for Mimi was like wading through a swamp and fending off a flock of gators trying to bite my kneecaps off. It ain't easy, and I could never figure out why.

Mimi always used a manual wheelchair. She could never have used a "wheelchair from a box." That was the kind Medicaid always pushed on her. She could never have had a powered one, either. They are super-duper expensive — as in the price of a small car. Mimi was not aware of gravity and would have gone over a curb and tipped over in a heartbeat. Mimi could push herself around a little, but basically was along for the ride for someone to push her around.

After we first got a prescription from Mimi's doctor, the procedure went something like this: Rick, Mimi, and I would meet with a physical therapist and wheelchair vendor to determine her exact wheelchair needs, which would change every five years. Mimi had many issues with her twisty body that required custom padding, cushioning, and lots of other special supports. It felt like we were building a custom car. It was always a lively collaboration. I was amazed at the many innovations in the wheelchair world every five years. After figuring out what options needed to be built into the wheelchair, it was time for insurance to be filed.

Most employee insurance plans do not cover wheelchairs. Fair enough. I could understand that. One of Mimi's wheelchairs typically ran about $8,000. But if the employee plan did cover even a portion, Medicaid would pay for the rest. I have to say, having the employee insurance and Medicaid, while nice — and we wouldn't have had it any other way — always made things so much more complicated. It was like a dance, and difficult to know who was leading. First, I would file with Rick's employee insurance. When that coverage was known, Medicaid was filed. In theory, it sounds simple.

But the wheelchair never took as long to build as it took for the medical insurers to get their act together. And a parent had better know what stage of approval things were in, or the ball got dropped — a lot.

It was the very last wheelchair Mimi owned that was the most challenging. It was partly Hurricane Harvey's fault. But there were other obstacles that were difficult to pinpoint. The roadblocks made no sense, since Mimi had had at least six wheelchairs in her lifetime. Approval for a manual wheelchair that should have taken a couple of months wound up taking ten months.

When I first met with the wheelchair vendor, he said Mimi would have a new wheelchair in eighty-four days. I laughed at him when he told me that and put the date down on my Outlook calendar. I remember telling him I would make him a quilt and a batch of homemade cookies if that happened. It took exactly 364 days for the chair to be delivered. It might have taken longer, but again, divine intervention happened. Mimi was one day reassigned to a lovely Medicaid caseworker who really helped move things along.

When Mimi's last wheelchair was delivered, there was a wide strip of camo on the upper back. It was totally not for a girl. I just shook my head in disbelief. Really? The vendor asked if I wanted the wheelchair returned. I refrained from screaming "No!" Of course, we kept it. Several people told me the camo fit Mimi perfectly since she was fierce. I had to ponder that comment for many moments. Obviously, Mimi was fierce in the way she sought out people to hug. If you locked eyeballs with Mimi, it was all over. You were going to get one of her fierce hugs. She never wanted to let go. Maybe that is what they meant.

In the past, I had always donated her old wheelchair, as it always had some life left in it. But by the time Mimi finally got this last new wheelchair, the old one was so awful — it was now six years old — we left it at the curb for heavy garbage pickup. That really broke my heart.

Mimi only had her new wheelchair a few months before she left us. I donated it to the Texas Paralyzed Veterans. The lovely man who picked Mimi's wheelchair up for donation was a veteran. He said it would go to someone who needed it. Perhaps the camo was divine intervention.

That last wheelchair retaught me to be hyper-persistent and never give up on the mission. But it just shouldn't be that hard to acquire a new wheelchair for a person who clearly used one their entire life.

—

As Mimi grew older, and heavier, transportation eventually became a huge issue. For years, I just lifted a slight little Mimi like a ten-pound bag of potatoes into the back seat and strapped her into a car seat. She was light. Until she was six or seven, the wheelchair stroller could be folded and lifted into the back of a car. Easy peasy.

When our kids were little, we purchased a Suburban we called the family truckster. By then, Mimi had an actual wheelchair and she could wheel herself around if she wanted. But mostly, we wheeled her around. Mimi could still be lifted into the back seat, but now the wheelchair was an issue. It was too bulky and awkward for one person to lift into the back of the car.

My engineering husband devised a way to have a scooter lift installed. Then he designed a docking device for Mimi's wheelchair. He also designed a hook-type bracket that attached to the lift. Rick found a local welder who made the docking device and bracket. Rick attached the docking device to the bottom of the seat on Mimi's wheelchair. It worked perfectly. The scooter lift had a handheld device with electrical control buttons that, once the wheelchair had the docking device attached, allowed me to lift it and swing it inside the back of the car. That scooter lift lasted as long as the Suburban — eighteen long years.

After the Suburban died, I got a smaller car. Katie and Ricky were out making their ways in the world. It was now just the three of us: Mimi, her dad, and me. Rick and I figured we were "strong like bulls" and could make my new car work for many years. We just had to change our lifting strategy. Hubby and I performed a two-person lift of Mimi from her wheelchair into the back seat of my car. We would then take her wheelchair apart (no easy feat) and place all the parts into the back of the car. Assembling them on the other end took practice, but we got rather good at it. The disassembly and reassembly also accelerated the wear and tear on the wheelchair. We made this work for about four or five years.

When Rick received a cancer diagnosis in early 2016, we realized life was going to get difficult — fast. Our two-person-lift days were coming to a rapid close. I quickly started the process of finding a different mode of transportation so I could get Mimi and her wheelchair in a car easily by myself.

I found the perfect solution at a new car show. I talked the ear off a salesman who educated me about a modification to either a Honda or a Toyota where they lowered the chassis and took out the last row of seating. The back of the car opened, and there was enough clearance to roll a wheelchair inside the car. I also learned about a locking system that grabbed the bottom of the wheelchair (when fitted with a docking device) and locked it down. There were also manual tie-downs for added safety. The engineering husband loved safety features. The car's modifications would cost just over $20,000. Even though the car I drove was paid off, the investment would still be very substantial for our family. I totally understood why we tried to make do all those years without a new vehicle.

Fortunately, the state of Texas has a couple of benefits, but you are required to purchase a new vehicle and modify it for wheelchair accessible purposes. One benefit is that the vehicle's sales tax is waived. This helps. When we had purchased the Suburban new a couple of decades before, the waived sales tax actually paid for the scooter lift.

The HCS program in which Mimi was enrolled after being on the waiting list for thirteen years helped with the new vehicle's modification. It paid $10,000 of the cost, making Mimi's car much more affordable.

From start to finish, the accessible van took ten months to acquire. It wasn't as horrible as the wheelchair process, but nearly. I don't want to even relive it here. I'll save it for if I write a sequel.

Chapter Fifteen
The Simple Life

Today me live in the moment, unless it's unpleasant,
in which case me will eat a cookie.
— Cookie Monster

I believe a child who is so dependent on someone having to dress, feed, bathe, potty, and transport them eventually develops extreme patience. Mimi did lots of waiting and did it heroically. At home, she waited for a meal to be brought to the table, waited for me to lift her out of bed in the morning, waited for me to wipe that cute little face clean of food shrapnel after breakfast, and waited for someone to get her on and off the school bus. Lots of waiting for stuff to be done to her and for her. You get my drift.

There is a sign in American Sign Language for the word "wait." Since Mimi didn't always "enunciate" her signing perfectly, I can only assume her translation of the sign was the accepted version. Mimi's sign resembled her two little hands clenching and unclenching.

It was the same with her unconventional signing of colors. But everyone in our family knew exactly what she was signing. When she was older, the verbalization of "wait" came out as "way." Endings of words were often dropped, and sometimes beginnings were changed to something easier — as in "Tadie" for Katie.

Guess I must have said "wait" a lot, also. If we were waiting on the little school bus to come to our house in the morning, I would tell her we had to wait. If I was getting Mimi ready to go somewhere, I might tell her we were going out for dinner. She would be so excited, and she expected it would happen in the next minute or two. When I told Mimi she would have to wait, she would throw up the "wait" sign but "say" it with both little hands in quick succession as if she was about to take off and fly. She never got upset. It was a patient and at the same time excited kind of waiting.

—

Mimi lived in the moment and was always looking forward to the very next one — literally. Basically, she really loved "going." To her, it was fun to go anywhere. It didn't matter if it was just around the block for a walk. That was totally fun for her. In fact, it was a grand adventure. Mimi and I might happen upon a cat or a dog barking somewhere out in the distance, and Mimi would react with giggles. Better yet, we might run into someone on our way around the block. They were always some of her very favorite people. Ceil might be gardening in the front yard. Her hugs were genuine and loving, hands covered with a light dusting of pungent earth like chocolate icing on a cake. Sometimes, Nancy would be looking out the window and run out the front door to give Mimi a hug. Those might be the days we didn't make it all the way around the block because we lingered, but we didn't care.

Mimi could be gone all day at school or at the day center, and when I would go out to retrieve her from the bus, the first thing she would say was, "mall, Donald's (short for McDonald's), Sonic?" She was always ready to go.

—

In 2015, I wrote a column for *The Tribune* about my version of a beautiful day in the neighborhood with Mimi.

The Tribune
You Gotta Laugh —
"A Beautiful Day in My Neighborhood"
Written by Dixie Frantz
Published February 25, 2015

There is a tree that grows on the corner of a busy intersection in my neck of the Livable Forest. I keep a close right eyeball on it this time of year. The skinny trunk is all crooked and gnarly. It looks mighty pitiful most of the year. But as in years past, the tree finally expressed itself recently. The ends of its thin branches bloomed all over with thousands of delicate white flowers. It is how I know spring must be just around the river bend. Of course, you wouldn't know that if you lived in the frozen northeast. I suspect there is a contingent in Boston that would love to ring the neck of that darn ground hog right about now!

The hint of recent sunny weather and mild temperatures has teased my special needs daughter and me into daydreaming of a leisurely stroll around our block. Over the decades, I have worn out many pairs of tennie runners and wheelchair tire treads with the number of times the two of us have made the trek. The round trip takes about 30 minutes ... unless we meet some neighbors along the way. Then Mimi and I could be gone an hour or more. My husband says I was vaccinated with a phonograph needle. Obviously, my nice neighbors and I were immunized by the same physician.

In decades past, our youngest loved to accompany us. Back then Mimi had a simple wheelchair stroller with a large metal plate to plant her teeny feet on. Ricky musta been about two when he started to accompany us. After a few minutes of strollin', Ricky would ask if he could ride. He then perched on the metal plate between Mimi's feet, leaned back, and just enjoyed the scenery. Pretty soon, Mimi would reach down and tug on the front of Ricky's hair, pulling his head slowly back and then releasing. Ricky never complained. For him, it was like throwing a wad of quarters in the toll road bin. It is the price you pay to ride with your sister.

The past couple of years, I started something new. Pushing Mimi's wheelchair down the driveway, I sing a little ditty, kinda softly. Don't want anyone to think I've totally lost my noodle.

"It's a beautiful day in the neighborhood, a beautiful day for a neighbor, won't you be mine, could you be mine ... won't you be my neighbor," my version of Mr. Rogers, only without the sweater.

Mimi and I are so thankful for wonderful neighbors. Drake lives across the street and is always ready to wave a huge hello with his whole arm. He is in first grade now and reminds me of Ricky twenty years ago.

Did I tell you the story of when Drake and his friend were raising money? A few months ago, they came to our front door selling pink lemonade ... for donations only. Their goal was to raise money to buy a chair for their "workshop." I love a couple of dudes with an honorable goal. After his impressive sales pitch, I planted five dollars in his little hand. It was totally worth the squeals. I suspect Drake has a serious future in sales.

Just a few doors down the street is Nancy's house. If she happens to be looking out the kitchen window as we are about to pass, Nancy runs out her front door and gives Mimi the biggest hug. Nancy's flowers are the best on the block. She inspired me to plant a flat of pansies just before winter set in. Green thumbs I do not have, but I gotta say most of my pansies are still hangin' in there.

Further down the block, if Ceil is out, there are more hugs flying back and forth. Her front yard looks like a magnificently wild and wonderful manicured jungle growing all kinds of interesting leafy things that I *couldn't identify if you paid me. She is the nicest lady on the planet and a Master Gardener ... an awesome combination.*

When Mimi and I finally make it over to the next street, there is this nice lady that has taught piano lessons in her home for years. She has a lovely fluffy dog and spends lots of time snuggling up her dog close to Mimi so she can give it a proper pet.

That Mr. Rogers had it right ... it really is all about the people you meet in your neighborhood. Let's hope the folks in the deep-freeze Boston area thaw soon so they can hug the neck of their neighbor!

—

There is a certain wonderfulness about being in the moment. I imagine heaven to be just like this — free from regret about the past or worry about the future. Mimi taught me that in so many simple quiet moments: walking around the block, holding her hand in church, sharing a messy and delicious chocolate chip cookie at the mall before a movie, or brushing her long, thick hair in front of the mirror. They were some of the finest and truest Mimi moments.

Mimi had a handful of favorite things. She loved the old black-and-white *Dennis the Menace* series. For a bunch of years, the Dennis DVDs were not available. I was always on the lookout for them, and when they came up for sale, I purchased all the seasons. They were her favorite to watch while eating her pancakes in the morning.

There were McDonald's French fries, *Rugrats* cartoons, *Wheel of Fortune* (especially the 'dorable Vanna), and Barney the big purple dinosaur. When the weather wasn't too hot, we walked around our long block, probably several hundred times in thirty-four years.

Mimi loved people — all people. Well, she particularly loved Santa, but that is a whole other story. Mimi did not see race, religion, class, and most especially, disability. Everyone was equal in her big blue eyes. Deacon James, a deacon from St. Martha's many years ago, told me Mimi would look straight into his eyes as if she were looking into his very soul. He felt it. I believe him. I have had the same experience.

As Mimi got older, Fuddruckers was her favorite eating spot, mostly because of the cute busboys who cleared off the tables. She ate off the kids' menu. Fuddruckers also worked for Rick and me much better than regular fast food. We could get our own grown-up meal. It was a win-win situation. Mimi loved their grilled cheese sandwiches. Rick and I could eat a nice burger. But she also loved family pizza night on most Fridays (a lovely cheese pizza was her favorite, just like Kevin from the movie *Home Alone*). I miss Mimi's Friday pizza night.

Mimi also loved her Tex-Mex. Set in front of her a plate of refried beans (not spicy) and rice (properly blown on by her mom so it wasn't too hot), and Mimi would devour the whole kid's plate. All I had to do was mix the beans with the rice and hand her a spoon in her left hand. She was a little messy, but with an occasional discreet swipe of that cute little face she was back in business to plow further down the plate.

—

I also learned so much from Mimi about the power of a hug. I believe it was her gift and a way of serving others. Many years ago, there was an old man named Andy who sat way across the church from us every week. He walked slowly, and his clothes were all wrinkly and baggy. For several decades, I wheeled Mimi over to him after Mass so she could give him a hug. She always hugged him carefully so as not to knock him down. I guess she sensed he was a little fragile.

Shortly before Andy died, the two hugged at Mass for the last time. Until then, in all those years, I had never heard Andy say a word. I remember telling Andy that day that Mimi so looked forward to hugging him every week. I don't know what made me say it. He smiled and whispered, "I look forward to her hugs also." He certainly looked like a man who wasn't hugged very often, but needed it more than most. And it was obvious Mimi knew. In fact, she always picked out certain people.

What Mimi lacked physically and in other areas, she made up for socially and spiritually. Hugging was Mimi's true gift, although she didn't hug every person who entered her sphere of influence. On occasion Mimi was picky. I believe it was also her mission in life to hug as many people as possible — at least the worthy ones.

—

When our kids were little, I was always trying to figure out how to do things together. There are seven years between my oldest and youngest. We went to the zoo and museums, but you can't do that every day. It is how I came up with the idea of turning a mundane task like grocery shopping into an adventure. I usually tried to pick a time of day when there wouldn't be lots of people shopping.

In the beginning, Katie pushed Mimi down the aisles of the grocery store. Mimi loved it when Katie would give her something to pitch into the cart I was pushing. Ricky was usually busy checking out the lobsters in the seafood department or begging the bakery lady for another free cookie. Eventually, Ricky would reunite with us — strangely about five minutes before I was ready to ask the checkout lady to call for him on the intercom to find his mother.

As Ricky got a little older, he delighted in pushing, and sometimes running, Mimi in her wheelchair around the store while Katie and I filled the shopping cart. I can still hear Mimi squeal. I also recall the large wire cage of bouncy balls in one corner of the store. Ricky loved to take one of the large balls and bounce it back and forth to Mimi. It is a wonder we were not banned from the store, or at the very least Ricky.

We also loved going to the movies. When the kids were little, it was a family affair. As Katie and Ricky ran off sprinting into the world, oftentimes my mom went with Mimi and me. I'd always lift Mimi out of her wheelchair to a bottom row so she could sit close to me. We shared a bag of popcorn and a Coke. Mimi loved all the kiddie movies. If a movie dragged a little in places, she would start humming. I would distract her with more popcorn and Coke.

One year Mimi and I saw *Mamma Mia!* three times. There wasn't much out that year that Mimi could watch on the big screen, and personally I loved that movie. There was lots of happy music and dancing, always a big hit with Mimi.

The whole movie experience was exciting to her. It was the only time I could sit close to her and not have a wheelchair between us. It was so different than just holding her hand at church or sitting next to her at the dinner table. This was cuddling close and I loved it — a deep and personal connection. I couldn't be certain Mimi felt the difference, but she sure did giggle a lot while grabbing popcorn from our bag.

—

Our family liked to occasionally hang out at the bowling alley. Back in the day, there weren't very many family activities in which Mimi could also participate, but bowling was one of them. Before bowling alleys got the hint and invested in movable ramps for those in wheelchairs, one of them provided us with a plastic kiddie slide. It wasn't the safest ramp to push a bowling ball down, but we made it work. We always made sure to add bumpers to the lane for Mimi. I enjoyed sharing her lane, as I can't bowl worth a flip! Yep, we were bowling buddies too.

When it was Mimi's turn to roll the ball down the ramp, Katie and Ricky took turns setting up the slide, and her dad carefully placed the bowling ball at the top of the slide. At Mimi's slight little push, the ball would careen down her alley. Often, Mimi received the top bowling score. She would not learn to high-five until many years later, but she always squealed and clapped with delight after the pins started falling down like dominoes.

Mimi started bowling at the Village Learning Center once a week, and to say it was her favorite activity is an understatement. Her bus driver, Mr. Ron, taught Mimi to high-five.

—

She also loved Sonic. No one is ever going to say Sonic has healthy and nutritious food. It is clearly fast food, and it was just something her parents were going to have to accept. Once I figured out Mimi loved the whole Sonic experience, we made it a routine. For several years, Sonic turned into a habit after 11:00 a.m. Mass. For Mimi, each time I pulled into the stall and pushed the button to order, it was like the very first time. It was that exciting to her.

We would swing by and grab something to go for Mimi. She adored their grilled cheese sandwiches and French fries. She loved waiting for the car hop to bring her kid's meal. I would hand the bag over to Rick. He would cool one of the hot fries in front of the air-conditioning vent and then hand it back to Mimi. I feel certain the fries must have tasted best in the back seat. Four fries later and we were home. I would set her meal up with her favorite DVD, cutting her sandwich so she could finger-feed herself, and pour her drink halfway into one of her cups. She was in heaven! Mimi didn't have a lot of choices she could make. That is probably why we caved when it came to Sonic.

Getting Mimi's hair cut was often a challenge. There were transportation issues. I had to consider curb cutouts and wheelchair ramping and needing to combine trips. I sometimes used random haircutting places at the mall so I could combine shopping with a haircut. I didn't want to take Mimi in and out of the car several times in a day. Mimi was heavy, and lifting her in and out of a wheelchair made it more challenging. It didn't matter what car I was driving. In general, it was a tedious and back-breaking process.

Mimi loved the idea of getting her hair cut. It meant being social. When it came to a pair of sharp scissors approaching a tress of her hair, I made sure to assist. Keeping Mimi from turning around to see what everyone in the room was doing was a challenge. I was determined to come out of the place with a decent haircut for Mimi.

I decided early on to make it a teachable moment for everyone — for Mimi and the person cutting her hair. I figured if I could train a bunch of hairdressers it was not scary to cut hair for our special needs population, then everyone won. So, if Ricky was getting his haircut at the barbershop, so was Mimi. If we were at the local mall, Mimi got her haircut at one of the mall's walk-in salons. Sometimes, I would take her to my hairdresser if I was anticipating a big change in her hairdo, like cutting off several inches. Oh, and I always handed the tip to Mimi to give to the hairdresser or barber.

Did I mention that I don't cut hair? It all has to do with my dad. When I was a first-grader, my mother had one of those haircutting kits that allowed her to buzz-cut my two brothers' heads. There were sharp scissors for the girls. For some reason, this one time, my mom was having a terrible time with my bangs. It was the very beginning of the summer. Every time she made another pass with the scissors, my bangs were still crooked. Suddenly, my dad said he would try. Now, my dad NEVER cut hair. I don't think he ever did again after what he did to me. The next day my mom took me to an actual hairdresser. I entered the salon with a scarf on my head. You should have seen the look on the stylist's face when I took it off! All she could offer was to even things out and do some shaping. And that is how the first pixie haircut was born. Bet you didn't know that. It was still awfully short when I started school in the fall.

As Mimi advanced in years, and particularly the year when Rick was going through cancer treatment, it was harder and harder to tend to Mimi's long tresses. My hairdresser, Lien, was the one who taught me the haircutter's secret of how to cut Mimi's bangs.

I would wheel Mimi into the kitchen where it was well lit, lay a towel in her lap, and wet down her bangs with a comb. As Lien had taught me, I would bring all of Mimi's bangs to the center of her forehead, right between her eyebrows, and snip with sharp scissors. Afterward, when the hair was laid out along her forehead, it was perfect, longer at the temples and straight across the eyebrows. It was probably a year or two before I got the nerve to have Lien teach me to thin Mimi's thick bangs.

I am forever grateful to Lien for crushing all my hair emergencies. She opened the shop early, at eight a.m., so I would have more time in my short day to get things accomplished before Mimi was picked up from the day center. I am also so thankful she understood how difficult it was for me to have Mimi come for haircuts often. Lien even came to our house on a Sunday to cut Rick's hair when I couldn't get him into the salon due to a huge cancer setback.

—

There was a funny side to Mimi. There is a children's story entitled "The Grumpy Bug," written by Robert Scull. My favorite version is online, narrated by Sandra Bernhard. Mimi and I used to enjoy the super-short video hunched over my iPad and would just crack up. She enjoyed it her entire life.

It is about a youngster bug with a bad attitude. His mother sends the grumpy bug out to play. The grumpy bug demands all the bugs that pass him by play with him. Of course, they all refuse and leave the bug alone. After all, no one wants to play with a grumpy bug. The grumpy bug says "grrrr" throughout the video, which always made Mimi smile. Rejected by three friendly flies, two blue bugs, and a sleepy snail, the grumpy bug finally starts to jump in the puddles and bounce on some mushrooms. His attitude suddenly changes, and he starts to laugh. He is having fun. And just like that, the grumpy bug suddenly becomes happy. When the flies, the two blue bugs, and the snail happen to pass by again, they notice the grumpy bug's attitude has changed. They ask the grumpy bug if he wants to play with them, and he does. I love a happy ending.

Now, why am I telling you this grumpy tale? It is one of those inside stories that all families have, like me and my grandson, Ben, and our secret high five. On the rare occasion that Mimi would act the least bit grouchy, I would ask her if she was being a grumpy bug. Her response? "Grrrr" ... and a laugh.

—

There were times when we didn't all laugh. I recall Christmas shopping was especially difficult as Mimi became an adult. I finally resorted to purchasing clothing — she had plenty — and wrapping everything in separate boxes. She loved to unwrap presents.

One year in early December, Katie called me from Target. She had been wandering up and down the toy aisles for an hour. I could tell she was crying. After trying to calm her down, I asked her what was wrong. Katie was struggling with what to buy Mimi for Christmas. Out poured all the emotions we both felt. Then I started to cry. Mimi was mentally a two-year-old but physically an adult. It was not appropriate to buy her toys, but she would probably love nothing more than toys for a two-year-old. Maybe.

The worst part? Mimi couldn't tell us what she wanted. Every year we just guessed. I don't recall what Katie finally got Mimi that Christmas. I think it was clothes. On the other hand, my mother gifted Mimi the latest talking Elmo — Chicken Dance Elmo. You push a hidden button on Elmo's little toe, and he sings and flaps his "wings." It was Mimi's favorite toy for ten years.

After that life lesson, Katie and I decided, to heck with this! If we wanted to purchase a cute toy for Mimi, that is what we did.

—

Mimi knew many Santa stand-ins for the real Santa over the decades. However, she never learned to enunciate the word "Santa." Some multisyllable words were just too darn difficult. But when Mimi articulated her verbal version of Santa, she called him "Ho-Ho," and everyone knew exactly what she meant.

From the time Mimi sat on her first Santa lap in the mall, she was delightfully enchanted. Something about this Santa dude was special. Not so special to her little brother Ricky. He rained down tears on Santa's lap when he was about three. But Mimi and her big sister, Katie, were delighted to be in Santa's presence.

I have so many Santa stories where Mimi is concerned. When Katie was five, and Mimi was one, there were lots of kids about the same age on our block. We also had the perfect portly neighbor with a booming voice. Sam had his own Santa suit and dressed up for several years until he moved away. Santa's true identity was top secret! On Christmas Eve, Santa would travel from house to house and sprinkle his Santa magic on all the little kids.

Another one of my Santa memories with Mimi was a chance encounter at a little festival. I was wheeling Mimi around a corner, and there he was — Santa — on his way to his sleigh. Perched in her wheelchair, Mimi lifted her little arms, tensed up, and loudly squealed. Santa did the same and approached Mimi. The two hugged for a full minute before both let go, exhausted. I never knew who was under the red-and-white suit, but he was the perfect Santa that night.

For many years, several moms with special needs children organized a Christmas party at our local YMCA. Santa was part of the program, complete with sleigh, cute little teenagers dressed up as elves, and photos donated by a local photographer. Mimi's YMCA photo with Santa was always the same. Mimi preferred to stare lovingly into Santa's eyes instead of looking into the camera.

One year, Mimi was not able to attend the YMCA Christmas party. She was recovering from orthopedic surgery over the school Christmas break. I don't know how Sparky, that year's Ho-Ho, found out. He told me his sleigh would be stopping by our house, complete with elves and presents. There are people in this world with the kindest of hearts. Sparky has always been one of those special ones.

Many years later, I worked part-time at a local hotel for a couple of years, in the back office. It was a great little job. Jeb drove the hotel van, and sometimes we had the opportunity for a little chitchat. He was also a Vietnam Veteran and lover of cats and dogs and a heart for those with special needs. Every year, he grew out his beard and played Santa for the local dog shelter. I would tell him stories about our Mimi and how much she loved Santa. When a few months later the hotel's annual Christmas party came up, Rick, Mimi, and I attended. I think Jeb was as surprised as Mimi about the sparks that flew that night. They both exploded with Christmas magic and threw it into the air like golden glitter.

From that moment on, for ten years, Jeb came to our house every Christmas Eve. He would stay for a spell, mostly hugging and un-hugging Mimi multiple times. Jeb always called me about a month before Christmas to let me know he was thinking of Mimi and to ask if it was okay for him to come on Christmas Eve.

In later years, a few neighbors, relatives, and our two grandsons were able to witness the magic of Santa up close and personal along with Mimi. When Mimi left us in October 2018, Jeb was one of the first people I called. I did not want Jeb to call me and to have to explain why I had not called one of Mimi's favorite people on the planet. To Mimi, maybe Jeb was Santa, but I felt certain she might also have understood that Jeb and Santa overlapped. He would want to know.

The first Christmas without Mimi was so difficult. She had only been gone two months. Obviously, the magic had gone out of the air for us in 2018. It was stifling. Our Santa tradition with Jeb needed to stay in the past. We would have to make new memories, but would never forget the special ones our neighbors and extended family had witnessed. It was truly an example of the magic of Christmas in the hugs of a special Santa and Mimi.

I've written many columns for the newspaper over the years about Mimi and her relationship with Santa. Below is one of my favorites, from 2016, which appeared in *The Tribune*. I think Mimi would have liked it.

The Tribune
You Gotta Laugh — "Ho-Ho Is His Name"
Written by Dixie Frantz
Published December 5, 2016

It is no secret our special needs daughter loves Santa. I mean she REALLY LOVES Santa. Ask anyone who has been around Mimi this time of year. They will certainly nod their heads in total agreement. Over the years, lots of us have had the experience of being treated like a large piece of stinky chopped liver when Santa makes an appearance in Mimi's general vicinity.

It doesn't help that there are kindly gentlemen everywhere donned in Santa suits sporting fluffy white beards, real or fake. Of course, I think we can all agree the real Santa needs all the help he can muster getting ready for the big day. I was in the local garden center yesterday purchasing a couple of bedding plants when Santa walked up pulling a little wagon loaded up with bags of mulch. I love how this time of year Santa is out there spreading my kind of Christmas cheer. I mean ... how can you not smile?

And over the years, we have had many encounters with such awesome Santa dudes. There have been lots of "mall" Santas for sure. You have to give them credit. It has gotta be a tough job with all that crying and carrying on. You would think the little kids were visiting their pediatrician for a check-up and a shot, instead of a photo and a candy cane.

My favorite mall Santa photo was snapped when our Ricky was little, probably two or three years old. While waiting in the line, Ricky was clearly projecting nervous vibes in Santa's direction. It didn't get any better when his two smiling sisters showed him how harmless the guy was getting their photo made with Santa. I'm not sure how I talked the hubster into sitting on Santa's lap with a crying Ricky, but we got the shot. Priceless.

It was probably thirty years ago when we had a neighbor on the block that dressed up as Santa. He went from house-to-house and paid all the kids a visit. His real name was Sam and he had this great booming voice. When Santa said, "ho-ho" you knew he meant business. It could have been that defining "Santa love" moment for our special child, Mimi, who is perpetually stuck mentally being two or three years old. To Mimi ... Santa will always be "Ho-Ho."

When Mimi was in middle school there was a special needs Christmas event she was going to miss. She was feeling fine but still recovering from orthopedic surgery. The Santa that year, his real name is Sparky, found out Mimi wasn't going to make it. So, before the party, Santa Sparky swung by our house, with all his "elves," AND brought a bag of presents. Who does that?

There is one special Santa that still pays Mimi a visit ... and on Christmas Eve night for the past ... I don't know how many years. He always calls me a couple weeks before the big day. Actually, Jeb missed one year when he broke his leg. And he felt really bad about not making it. Can you imagine? You should hear the way he says, "ho-ho-ho" under his breathe. It's pretty cool.

I met Jeb about ten years ago. He drove the shuttle bus at a local hotel. I worked part-time in the back office for several years. One day that first fall, Jeb told me about how every year he grew out his beard to play Santa ... and he owned three Santa suits. I'm serious.

It was that year at the hotel's Christmas party Mimi first met Jeb. Staff and their family were all invited to the festivities. I will never forget when we wheeled her wheelchair through the automatic doors. Jeb was all decked out in his Santa suit and handing out presents. When Santa and Mimi locked eyeballs, it was love at first sight.

And Santa Jeb has been coming to our house ever since spreading Christmas cheer and lots of hugs all around. Each year is a gift. I know one of these years I will not be getting that phone call that Jeb is able to come to see Mimi. He moved a few years ago and his health is not the best. But for all the times Santa Jeb has made it by our house to spread his special kind of joy ... I have to say ... it has been a privilege for me to play the part of stinky chopped liver.

The spirit of Santa Claus was an important part of Mimi's life. She couldn't have cared less about gifts. All she really wanted was a bunch of hugs from Ho-Ho.

Chapter Sixteen

A Scary Diagnosis

Cancer is not a straight line.
It's up and down.

— Elizabeth Edwards

In the fall of 2015, Rick and I began the search for an unknown health foe. We searched for several months for the medical reasons for Rick's coughing, extreme sinus drainage, and sudden ten-pound weight loss. When a lump popped up on his chest after Christmas, he had an ultrasound of the area. A local doctor at the small clinic said to just watch it and not to worry. It was probably nothing. I didn't like the sound of that answer. I promptly got a copy of the test and showed it to a doctor in the medical center. After a biopsy on Fat Tuesday, the day before Ash Wednesday, Rick was diagnosed with stage 2 breast cancer. This seemed ridiculous, as Rick had nine sisters, and none of them had ever had breast cancer.

Because of Rick's boss, Brett, we went elsewhere. Brett convinced Rick he needed an urgent second opinion. His company had a special cancer program with Houston's MD Anderson Cancer Center (MDA). Rick had worked for Shell for several years, but was not aware of the company's cancer benefits. After the second opinion at MDA, we would soon learn it was much worse.

Cancer quickly became one of the scariest words on the planet at our house during the year 2016. Rick was in bad shape. After a CT scan, it was confirmed he had stage 4 kidney cancer. Every day he felt worse. I wheeled Rick in a wheelchair into MDA to see our new oncologist, with Katie at my side.

That first appointment was chilling. Dr. Matthew Campbell, Rick's oncologist, gave us only two choices: an immunotherapy clinical trial, which might work, or hospice. Rick, of course, chose the clinical trial. But it wasn't that simple. First, he had to qualify for the trial. That meant a solid month of testing at MDA in various areas of the hospital. We went back and forth to MDA three to four times a week. It was grueling.

I made a vow to hold myself together and not let Mimi suspect there was anything wrong with her daddy. I kept her routine as normal as possible.

After Rick finally qualified for the two-year trial, we had a path forward. There would be immunotherapy infusions every two weeks, and the tumor in his left kidney would be removed in May of 2016. But first, there would be a few immunotherapy infusions to cool the tumor. Recovery from the surgery would be intense, but eventually the infusions would start back up. That plan did not happen in a straight line. There were lots of bumps in the road, as anyone on a cancer journey will let you know.

Our church's Prayer Quilt Ministry, of which I was a member, put a blessed men's quilt on the fast track. It contained lots of plaid fabrics in browns and blues. We brought it to all his infusion appointments to cover him in prayer.

Thankfully, Rick was a "super responder," which meant the trial started to beat back the cancer after just two infusions. Rick was improving every day. Some of the bumps in the road included coming off the trial after a year. The immunotherapy had started to negatively impact his pancreas. After that, Rick went two years without treatment, with periodic scans and follow-up visits with Dr. Campbell.

One of the first people I called after we received Rick's diagnosis was Kim. She was one of the ladies who founded the Village Learning Center, Mimi's day center. I imagined Rick's cancer was going to be a huge challenge. Little did I know how unbelievably difficult it was going to be. One challenge was that MDA wasn't down the street, and the many appointments were not going to fit neatly between the hours when Mimi was at the day center.

After talking to my newspaper editor, Cynthia, I quickly got the hint that cancer was not going to be like running a sprint. She told me it was more like a marathon. Maybe even multiple marathons.

Kim listened to me while I cried buckets of tears in her ear about how cancer and Mimi's care were going to be difficult. The first words out of her mouth were, "Whatever you need, we will do." She told me to pack an overnight bag for Mimi and leave it at Stoney Glen. She suggested I call Vince, who managed Stoney Glen. Mimi would always have a place to stay if there was a late appointment, or an emergency, or just whatever I needed for Mimi. Those kind words gave me confidence that I had help with Mimi. Over the next year, Rick had as many as forty appointments just to qualify for the clinical trial. It was quite a juggling act. Never in my wildest nightmares did I expect so many appointments, and that didn't even include numerous scans of his brain, bones, chest, and abdomen. There were countless blood draws, infusions lasting many hours, visits with his oncologist, and visits with other types of doctors.

Mimi loved going for respite at Stoney Glen. Over the years, she had stayed many times, usually for a few days at a time. She couldn't enunciate the words "Stoney Glen." She called it the "house."

Managing early and late appointments at MDA was difficult. It normally took just over an hour to make the one-way trip to MDA. As Rick's health improved, he was able to drive himself to and from appointments. However, he was not good at navigating the complications and stresses of a health system. On the other hand, I was an expert. Decades of caring for Mimi had taught me how to advocate and navigate and ask lots of questions. I found spots like the quiet rooms at MDA, where Rick could rest in a dark room in an easy chair between appointments and scans. I knew where the coffee shop was located, and all the different eating places.

When Rick had an early appointment, often for bloodwork, he would leave before six a.m. I would jump into the car at seven a.m., when Mimi's bus left our driveway, and then meet Rick at MDA. I could then navigate the rest of the day for scans and doctor visits.

The same happened in reverse when there were late appointments. Rick might have multiple scans in a day, which meant the last one might happen late in the day. I would get Rick all checked in and talk with clinic staff, and then leave by three p.m. to get back before Mimi's bus arrived at our driveway. This was our routine for a solid year, but Mimi never knew what was going on in our complicated cancer world.

Sometimes traffic would mess up my travel back to Kingwood. I could just place a call on my cell phone and ask Vince to take Mimi over to Stoney Glen after the day center. He would make sure Mimi got a snack, or even dinner, if it got really late. I don't know what I would have done without their help. As my grandson Ben always loved to say, "teamwork makes the dream work." He was wise beyond his three years.

Then there was our Shell family. I've always loved the "oil patch." Many years ago, I worked as a secretary for an oil and gas company. In my experience, they are some of the finest people on the planet. Rick worked for Shell Oil Company for several years and had the same experience. Their support was also so instrumental in helping us beat back cancer. Besides lots of meals, cards, and flowers, there were Brett and Rick's work buddies stopping by for a special kind of support.

After mentioning to Brett that Rick could no longer help me bathe Mimi, he offered to help. Just as when Rick or Ricky helped me bathe Mimi, we did it modestly. It is a little complicated — but not really. Basically, I staged everything. Mimi bathed in a bath chair that resembled a lawn lounge chair. I laid her on a thick towel on a bathmat in front of the tub and undressed her. She was discreetly covered with a towel. I then would have the volunteer come into the room and help with a two-person lift into the tub with the bath chair. The volunteer would turn around and leave the room while Mimi was bathed. After that, she was again covered with a towel while the tub was draining. Our trusty volunteer would be called in to help with another lift onto the towel in front of the tub and again would leave. Are you seeing how it was done yet?

It took a little time to dry her off and get Mimi dressed as she lay on the floor, but after so many years, I was an expert. It was unfortunate she did not have the trunk control to sit up to help perform these activities, but we made it work. One more lift from the volunteer after Mimi was dressed, to get her back into her wheelchair, and we were done. Of course, Mimi always demanded a huge hug and squealed as her way of thanking the volunteer.

In fact, not only did Brett help, but he let Rick's work buddies know of our need. Many of them did not live close. After about a month, I decided these lovely people would not be able to drive long distances to help on a long-term basis. As we got deeper into cancer, I learned it might be many months before Rick would be helping me with lifting.

I started thinking that a longer-term solution to bathing Mimi was going to be a must. I couldn't impose on our rotation of awesome Shell dudes to help several times a week with Mimi forever. I needed an alternative.

I had attended a three-day ACTS retreat (ACTS stands for "adoration, community, theology and service") at our church some time before and called the lady who led our retreat. I didn't tell Acenith what I wanted when the request for coffee was initiated. We met at our local Starbucks and I started out slow. First, I laid out our family struggle with cancer and how this was going to be a challenge when it came to the care of Mimi. I warned her my request was going to be unusual and asked her to hear me out.

Next, I told her my need ... a strong guy a couple of nights a week to help bathe Mimi. You should have seen the look on her face. I thought she might run for the exit. Asking for her patience, I explained what exactly I meant by "bathing Mimi."

Once I explained that Mimi's bathing was performed modestly at all times when a dude was in the room, she got it. She put out feelers, and we had a lineup of strong men who helped for several months. I also had my awesome son-in-law on the weekends.

I was so thankful for Acenith's assistance. She made my very unusual request happen. A couple of months of assistance from some awesome Catholic men helped our family so much. Several months later, Rick was able to take over again.

It is grueling battling cancer. I was relieved to have a solution for how to care for Mimi during those unpredictable days.

I still cry when someone tells me they have just been diagnosed with cancer. Someone once told me that when a family member is diagnosed with cancer, it is the whole family that has it. I believe it.

However, I don't cry when someone tells me they have a child with special needs. Mimi has made my life so full. Cerebral palsy is not a terminal disease. I do immediately want to hug them, though, and let them know it is going to be challenging — but okay. Then I let them pick my brain for tips, tricks, and all the things I have learned over the years.

Chapter Seventeen

Our Lives Sadly Change Forever

If there ever comes a day when we can't be together,
keep me in your heart. I'll stay there forever.

— Winnie the Pooh

Mimi had a cold, and with it came a very stuffy nose. I could always immediately tell when Mimi had a cold, because she stopped humming. She hummed a lot. One long constant note. I don't know how she did it. Then came the more than usual mouth breathing. Since she was terrible at taking medication, my typical way of easing her stuffed little nose was to use a cold vaporizer. Just a few nights with a vaporizer usually knocked her stuffy nose to the curb. It was a beautiful thing. She had a strong immune system and rarely was sick.

Getting through those few nights of a bad cold was a challenge, mostly because of how she slept. Maybe it had to do with the pressure on her twisty spine, but Mimi preferred to sleep on her stomach, like a little baby. No pillow. The contractures in her knees meant she slept with her legs in the air from the knees down. Mimi also curled her two arms under her body. The challenge with a cold was all the snot and mouth fluids that accumulated on her sheet. I tried lots of ways to not let the sheet get too wet, placing pads under the sheet to absorb the moisture and going into her room at night and moving her from a wet spot to a dry one. You name it, I tried it.

This time I tried something different. The first night of her cold, I had her sleeping on her back, with her little head resting on a pillow. Then I propped pillows under her knees so she would be comfortable on her back. I covered her body loosely with a blanket and checked on her an hour later. She was asleep, with the vaporizer hissing on the floor of her room.

I was so happy when I went into her room the following morning. Mimi awoke refreshed, with no snot to be found anywhere. She was happy, still stuffy, and not humming. I told Mimi that one more night on her back with the vaporizer and she should be fine.

The second night, I washed, rinsed, and repeated, placing her on her back with carefully tucked pillows and a blanket. I checked on her around nine. She was sound asleep.

That fateful night, I never heard a noise coming from her room. I was always a light sleeper. But did I sleep deeply that night? Her room was in the back of the house. Our room was in the front. Why did I not hear her? I knew what the sound of banging on her wooden guardrail sounded like. When she was little, Mimi would sometimes throw all her stuffed animals out of her bed onto the floor. I knew exactly what that sounded like, too. Was the vaporizer loud enough to muffle her movements? I have asked myself this question a thousand times. I stood in front of her bed a hundred times after she left us, trying to figure out what happened. Were all the evils from Pandora's box let loose that night in Mimi's room? It just didn't make any sense.

I remember entering Mimi's room, as I did every weekday, at six a.m. on the dot. Mimi and I had our weekday routine down. It took me exactly one hour to get her ready for the day center bus. This included chatting about what she would do that day, a little potty sitting time, dressing, teeth and hair brushing, and chowing down on pancakes with a glass of milk. Lastly, Mimi would throw her last piece of pancake to the dog before the bus arrived at seven bells.

Wednesday morning, October 17, 2018, was profoundly different. As I entered her room, I came face-to-face with an unbelievably horrific sight. Instead of finding Mimi lying on her back in her bed as I had left her the night before, she had somehow slipped during the night, or early morning, between the guardrail and the mattress. But the gap was so very small. How could that happen? A couple of inches at best. I could not believe what I was seeing. Mimi looked as if she was sitting on the floor, with her hands at her side, against the bed. Her head was leaning back between the guardrail and mattress. She was so still.

I ran the few steps over to her, grabbed the guardrail and threw it onto the bed. I then took hold of her little shoulders and gently eased her body onto the floor, parallel with her bed. Touching her sweet face, I told Mimi to wake up. It proved futile. Her skin was cold and had a blue tinge to it. And her face. It was so peaceful, like she was asleep and would awake at any moment.

I ran into the kitchen to grab my cell phone and call 911, then ran back into Mimi's room. With the phone on speaker, the female voice calmly told me to perform chest compressions on Mimi and count with her. Every now and then I muttered "Oh Mimi." When I got to over two hundred chest compressions, the doorbell finally rang. I ran from the back of the house to unlock the front door. I showed the EMS (emergency medical service) personnel where Mimi's room was located. They entered her room, motioning for me to stay back. Thirty seconds later, they came out of the room and confirmed Mimi was gone.

It was then I called Rick at work and, with a quivering voice, told him to come right home. He became hysterical, and I feared for his safety. It was a forty-five-minute drive from his office. I prayed his guardian angel would watch over him.

One of the EMS men suggested that someone should probably drive him, but Rick said he wasn't going to wait. An EMS lady sat me down on the couch. She asked me if I knew someone to call to sit with me. I called my sweet neighbor Marie, who was dropping her son off at school. She would be right over.

A couple of Houston police arrived shortly after the EMS. The police let me know that sometimes the medical examiner does not come. I didn't know what that meant.

Then I called Katie at home. I knew she and Chad were getting their little boys ready and about to head out the door. I told Katie to go into another room and sit down. I didn't want her to be in the room with Jacob and Ben when I told her about her sister. I heard her voice quiver as I spoke the words of what happened. Katie started to sob. We were both sobbing. Katie and Chad live in Houston, about forty-five minutes away. She drove over to our house while Chad took the boys to school. Chad followed a little while later.

I called Ricky in Michigan, but it went to voicemail. I texted him to call me as soon as possible and called Kate, his wife. Then I recalled that his work doesn't allow cell phone calls. Kate called the landline to his operations floor and someone else answered. They told him to call his wife outside on his cell phone. Kate broke the news to Ricky as he stood outside his building. He was on the next flight to Houston.

Marie quietly sat with me on the couch in the living room. We just looked at each other and shook our heads in disbelief. When Rick came in the back door, Marie quietly left out the front door.

Rick went to Mimi's room and loudly sobbed. I had never heard such grief pour from his lips. He partially lifted her to his chest and just rocked her. Rick asked me to call Father TJ. It was still so early. He answered the church's phone number and came right over. Father TJ prayed with us over Mimi.

Rick asked one of the policemen if it was okay to move Mimi from the floor to her bed. He didn't want Katie to see her sister on the floor. Very carefully, Rick and I lifted Mimi's lifeless body to her bed, placing her head on the pillow and covering her up to her chest with her fluffy blue blanket.

The doorbell rang again. It was Mimi's bus driver, who had a strange look on her face. She was there to pick up Mimi for the day center. I just shook my head. I didn't tell her what happened. I couldn't say the words. She knew from the EMS and police vehicles it was something bad. She left without me being able to confirm the vehicles had anything to do with Mimi.

Katie came through the back door and headed straight back to Mimi's room. Lots of tears and disbelief. Chad, Katie's husband, followed through the back door sometime later.

At some point, two individuals from the medical examiner's office came to our house. Rick, Katie, and I were shooed out of Mimi's room. But Chad wandered down the hallway and stood outside Mimi's room while the two were taking photos. The Chicken Dance Elmo on Mimi's television shelf started squawking. Across the room, in Mimi's bed, another Elmo started talking. They didn't stop for a couple of minutes. The two Elmo dolls had not been touched. We believe it was Mimi. She was sending a message to those two medical examiner people that she didn't like them in her room. And we believe Mimi was also letting us know she was okay. I know it sounds unbelievable.

Finally, we were informed the medical examiner would be taking Mimi for an autopsy. They let us know it was something they did whenever there was a death in the home. It was not what we wanted to hear. The thought of Mimi being anywhere other than her home was too much to bear.

—

In the days preparing for Mimi's funeral, my husband and I thought about all that Mimi had left behind. I felt she had so much more to do on this planet. So many more people to touch. Don't we all have a legacy or two that define us? It was obvious to us that Mimi's legacy had to be her great big hugs. My lovely daughter-in-law, Kate, spent hours designing a two-sided card the size of a business card that was given out at the visitation and funeral. Since Mimi's death, I have given out many more to people who looked like they needed a hug. We may not be able to physically hug Mimi any longer, but we can pass her hugs on. And that brings me to Mimi's legacy and challenge to you.

One side of the card has a photo of Mimi bear-hugging Santa Claus around the neck, her beloved "Ho-Ho." The other side reads:

"Mimi's legacy was her ability to give the best hugs. We challenge you to pay it forward by giving someone a hug. Give them this card and encourage them to do the same, keeping the memory of Mimi's warm embrace alive."

—

I wrote a column for *The Tribune* that was published in 2018, after Mimi left us. It was the week of my yearly Halloween column that was not to be.

The Tribune
You Gotta Laugh — "Mimi's Legacy"
Written by Dixie Frantz
Published October 30, 2018

This week it was my intention to write a Halloween column before the unthinkable happened. It was going to be about trick-or-treating with two of our grand-munchkins. Ben and Jacob are the super-duper heroes saving the world from bad guys and needing lots of candy to complete their important mission.

But then ... life turned surreal in an instant. I am still hoping to wake up from the nightmare and it never happened. Our special needs daughter, Mimi, unexpectedly passed away. No words. Just extreme sadness at our house. In keeping with the title of this column, there will be moments of laughter ... and a few tears may spill.

Did you know Mimi LOVED Halloween? Not for the candy. Nope. It was about hugging the people giving out the candy. If she encountered a couple of pets in costume it was gravy on mashed potatoes. Of course, her parents LOVED the candy, and the lovely reactions of all the people that hugged our Mimi. She was a little girl mentally, trapped in a twisty body, confined to a wheelchair, and she hugged our neighbors ... for over 30 years.

There were also the yearly Halloween celebrations at the Village Learning Center. Mimi attended the awesome day center for the past dozen years since aging out of school. Monday was her favorite day of the week when her class went bowling. When I'd pick her up in the afternoon, I always asked if she beat the boys. The answer was always "Yeah!" with a high five. Our girl had a competitive side to her.

For the past few years at Halloween, I would dress her up as a princess with a tiara and hot pink extra-feathery boa. By the time Mimi returned from her day center festivities in the afternoon, she had just about picked the boa clean of all the feathers and her wheelchair backpack was full of candy. I always felt kinda bad about the cleaning people at the day center and their extra fluffy chores on Halloween.

Over the years, I've written quite a few columns about our Mimi. She was a little character that inspired me more than you can imagine. Mimi also challenged and kept me on my toes. At church most every Sunday, Mimi had this habit of requesting a run to Sonic just about the time everyone was praying the "Our Father." We never turned her request down. Little things matter. Perhaps I should consider going to confession for encouraging her. On second thought ... probably not.

Someone told me after Mimi's funeral that our daughter was an angel that had been on loan to us for a time. By the love from the hundreds of people that attended her visitation and funeral, I believe she was right. How is it that Mimi, a young lady with limited communication skills could touch so many people? If she made eyeball contact with you ... or you got close enough for her to grab your hand ... it was all over. Her arms were around your neck and I often had to pry them loose. Just ask every usher at our church. Yup ... you were getting a "Mimi hug" and you liked it.

This leads me to Mimi's Challenge: Mimi's legacy was certainly her ability to give the best hugs ... pure, simple and uniquely powerful. I challenge you to pay it forward by giving someone a hug, asking them to pass it on, and keep the memory of Mimi's warm embrace alive.

—

Besides being showered with meals, we received lots of beautiful flowers, lots of donations in Mimi's memory to the Village Learning Center, lovely cards, masses said for Mimi, and touching personal notes. St. Martha's Prayer Quilt Ministry donated several books about hugging to our children's library. Mimi would have loved that.

The Villagers at her day center wrote lots of little notes to the best of their abilities. One of these notes was signed by "God."

Mimi touched more people than I ever knew. Some of them very deeply. We sat in the front row at Mass for so many years. You just don't know what is going on in the hearts of those people who sit behind you. I can't tell you how many people still tell me they think about her more now than ever before.

—

I remember getting a call from the funeral home the day of Mimi's visitation. Mimi would have an open casket at the visitation and rosary. They wanted me to make sure her hair and makeup were what I expected. Could this get any worse? He had a photo of Mimi but wanted my approval. I had already told him Mimi never wore makeup, so I knew there would be no red lipstick or eyeshadow to deal with. My first reaction was to not go. Mimi's spirit was not in her body any longer. What did it matter?

After some reflection, I took along Katie and my daughter-in-law's mother, Aleta, for moral support and guidance. I could not do this alone. This was my first time to see Mimi since she left our home with the coroner.

The first thing I noticed was that cerebral palsy no long controlled Mimi's normally tense body. Her body looked so relaxed. It was very strange and unsettling. Where had she gone?

The hairdresser made a few adjustments, curling her bangs. Her long hair cascaded on both sides of her sweet little face. Her skin tone and lip color, a natural pale pink, looked fine. But there was something that didn't settle well. Mimi always had this toothy grin. Her two front teeth were a little long, and when she smiled, the ends of her front teeth hung over her bottom lip a little. Obviously, there was no way that signature look was going to happen. I asked the funeral director if they could apply a little makeup to make her top lip appear fuller. That little change made Mimi look more like herself.

Mimi held my and Rick's rosaries, one in each hand. We placed the prayer quilt Rick had received from our church's Prayer Quilt Ministry after his cancer diagnosis across the front of her casket.

We had a table covered with photographs and summer camp scrapbooks of Mimi, along with a huge bowl of M&M's, her absolute favorite candy. I can still feel Mimi's little fingers swipe across my palm as she picked them up one at a time.

There were so many people who filed through the funeral home for Mimi's visitation and rosary. There were lots of staff and Villagers from her day center, so many friends, family, parishioners, people from Rick's work, and community people. We were overwhelmed. Father Borski, who had retired, stopped by. Dr. Penn came to honor Mimi. Many of my quilting friends and several people from the newspapers for which I wrote stopped to pay their respects.

Deacon Jon Barfield led the rosary at Mimi's visitation. He was one of St. Martha's deacons who had hugged Mimi many times. As he stood at the podium leading the holy rosary, a screen behind him flashed lots of photographs of Mimi.

After the rosary, we invited anyone wanting to stay longer to join us on the adjoining patio. Everyone was given a glass filled with wine. A wine glass filled with chocolate milk sat on a concrete bench at the front of the patio facing the benches. Anyone who wanted to stand and share a story about Mimi was welcome. I declined, but Rick, Ricky, and Katie stood up to talk. There were several others who stood to talk about Mimi. After each story, there was a toast to Mimi. We all imagined Mimi was also toasting from heaven with her favorite drink ... chocolate milk. You would have loved her signature chocolate milk mustache.

—

It was a Monday morning at ten when Mimi's funeral Mass was held. Several hundred people attended. I was blown away. There were family members (close and distant), friends (close and distant), neighbors, parishioners, and teachers and staff from the Village Learning Center and Stoney Glen. There was a funeral Mass with Father TJ presiding and with Deacon James Meshell.

Deacon James was a deacon at a nearby parish. I don't know how he heard about Mimi, but he called us and asked if he could assist at her funeral Mass. He had been a deacon many years before at St. Martha's and had a special love for Mimi. Deacon James was one of Mimi's favorites.

We brought photos of Mimi and the picture books my mom had made her about Mimi's time at summer camp. Mimi had thumbed through these little scrapbooks hundreds of times. They were well loved and worn by Mimi. The camp scrapbooks told a different story about her life. There was also a large pottery bowl of M&M's.

It is still difficult for me to remember the funeral. I recall standing in the foyer of the church and people coming toward me. An old neighbor from down the street, Mollie, appeared at some point. Except for Facebook, I hadn't seen her in years. She came several hundred miles from the Dallas area. The lovely Heather and her mother also came from several hundred miles away. Family from California and Michigan flew in.

I had asked Clara to sing at Mimi's funeral. She has the most beautiful voice and also a member of our Prayer Quilt Ministry. Gayle also sang. She had known Mimi for many years and was one of Mimi's favorites to hug.

There was Vince from Stoney Glen, who oversaw the respite house. He hugged me tight, with huge tears in his eyes. He was my rock while Rick was going through cancer treatment. Then his staff, seven or eight or nine of them, entered the church foyer at the same time. We all got in a big circle and locked arms. There were so many amazing people who helped take care of Mimi so Rick and I could have a night away, or go on an adventure, or fight cancer.

—

Ten days after Mimi's funeral, I received a call from the coroner's office. Our Ricky and his family had already flown back to their home in Michigan. In writing their report, the coroner was struggling with the position of Mimi's body and wanted to do a "reenactment." I had already given them a statement twice of how I found her, but they were not entirely satisfied.

They placed this call on Halloween, which felt like a cruel joke, as it was Mimi's favorite holiday. We told them to come the following day, November 1, which was All Saints' Day. I made the appointment for the afternoon, as we have always attended Mass for the feast day. Our church had a Mass in the morning.

Katie drove from Houston to our house to be with us during the reenactment. Katie had been a teenager when CPS had turned our world upside down. She wanted to be a witness to whatever lay ahead with this latest chapter.

Three people came to represent the coroner's office. One was a photographer, one a social worker, and there was another individual from the coroner's office. I do not recall her title. They felt our unease at their presence and tried to tell us everything was okay. One of them told me they could tell our daughter was well cared for. Maybe it was the hallway that contained large photos of her fun times at camp. Maybe it was her room. A handmade quilt hung on one wall, a crucifix above her door, a television was in the corner, and her stuffed "babies" were lined up at one end of her bed. But you never know what people are really thinking.

I believe the issue was that, with the permission of the police, Rick and I had moved Mimi to her bed, placing her head on a pillow. I wasn't sure of anything anymore.

After describing to them again how I had found Mimi that horrible morning in her room, I was asked to position one of the coroner employees on the floor in that same spot. I was sick to my stomach. They didn't stay long. I knew the coroner had a hard job to do. It didn't mean I had to like it.

Chapter Eighteen

Difficult Days Ahead

The world breaks everyone and afterward many
are stronger at the broken places.

– Ernest Hemingway

In the Catholic Church, All Souls' and All Saints' days are celebrated a day apart. It was just a few weeks after Mimi had left us that Rick and I attended the holy day masses. We had attended these masses for as long as I can remember. Father Jonathan gave the homily for All Saints' Day.

Now, I have been a Catholic since I was nineteen years old. I was baptized into the Catholic Church the week before Rick and I were married. I had my first Holy Communion and the sacrament of matrimony on our wedding day. Rick liked to joke that I received three sacraments in a few days, while it had taken him over twenty-three years.

Regarding All Saints' Day, that would mean I had attended forty-six All Saints' Day masses. The basic message of Father Jonathan's homily, which I had never heard before, was that the holy day was for all those saints who have not been canonized by the Catholic Church. I had always thought it was celebrated only for the saints who were formally canonized by the church. It made me think — there are many saints in heaven who have not been canonized, and surely Mimi could be one of them.

—

The very formal coroner's report on what had caused Mimi's death was eventually emailed to me. It came about a month after Mimi died. It was a bit of a surprise. They had originally told us people sometimes do not receive the report for up to six months after a death.

I never opened the attachment. There was no way. I did learn after Rick read the report that Mimi's death was ruled an accident. That was a huge sigh of relief. We totally expected a terrible outcome with the coroner. Having a child with a disability is difficult for the outside world to understand. We knew the coroner was going to have a challenge writing the report. Someone in their office must have had some understanding of the life of a family with a special child and seen examples of how much we adored our Mimi.

Rick told me the coroner's report was multiple pages long. Rick and our son, Ricky, are the only ones to have read it. I am good with that. Rick told me only a few things about the report. He indicated it would indeed be too painful for me to read. He told me Mimi weighed 119 pounds. I never knew that. Her weight might have been the reason my left shoulder had started to ache. The report also stated Mimi was well taken care of. I am glad I did not read the autopsy report.

—

About a month after Mimi left us, three lovely young ladies who had worked with Mimi at her day center stopped by with dinner and gifts. The gifts were every ceramic piece at the day center that Mimi had touched with her painted fingertip, including multiple Christmas ornaments and a large serving platter. What precious gifts.

The day center had a kiln. Over the years, I have amassed a number of cute little ceramic plates for every holiday. Each plate featured Mimi's thumbprints.

The ladies also told me stories about Mimi. Mostly, we cried, but we also laughed.

—

In late 2018, I wrote a column for *The Tribune* about my encounter with the three special ladies at Mimi's day center who came to our home shortly after Mimi passed away.

The Tribune
You Gotta Laugh — "The M&M's That Bind Us"
Written by Dixie Frantz
Published November 27, 2018

M&M's, the little round color-coated candies, are pretty darn special at the Frantz house. A bunch of years ago my little sister, Gretchen, gifted our special needs daughter with a large M&M dispenser. She stuck lots of adorable Sesame Street character stickers like Elmo and Cookie Monster around the sides. Mimi's name is on the front of the clear base. On one side are the letters "Hands Off" which no one ever paid any attention to.

For years, it sat filled on her dresser like a slot machine ready to payout a multi-colored jackpot. All Mimi had to do was point in the dispenser's direction and I would gather a handful. I'd give them to her one at a time while she was watching her favorite television shows. The old black-and-white series Dennis the Menace, The Rugrats cartoons, or Home Improvement where some of her favorites.

The grandkids also adore M&M's. After bursting through the back door most every Sunday, it wasn't long before they would head to Mimi's room to raid her M&M's. She was very good at sharing. The boys also applauded her choices in television programming. Until recently, Jacob and Ben would stand on either side of her wheelchair for a spell to peek at what Mimi was watching.

Shortly before Mimi left us, two-year-old Ben came out of Mimi's room with his cheeks obviously filled with more than just his teeth.

"Do you have something in your mouth?" said the hubster, otherwise known as "Pop-Pop."

Ben just shook his head in the negative. A second later Ben grinned to reveal a mouth gushing with milk chocolate and multi-colored candy coatings. It is the reason we moved Mimi's M&M's to the kitchen. I predict the lad is destined to be the child that can't keep a secret ... or tell a lie.

Did I mention the hubster and I had some visitors for dinner about a week ago? Three very lovely ladies, Christina, Shaye and Erin, from the day center Mimi attended for many years, came bearing gifts and dinner. It was bittersweet with tears and laughter as we all shared stories about our special daughter who only weeks before was given her angel wings.

I think we all learned so much about Mimi that night. Since Mimi had a limited vocabulary and returned home each week with a backpack full of art and worksheets, I had assumed I knew how she spent her time at the day center. Shaye told us how she loved sharing her McDonald's French fries with Mimi.

Christina told us how Mimi sometimes liked to wander around the day center. If there was an open classroom door, Mimi would wander in and see what was going on. Sometimes she would wheel herself to the front desk to visit. Often there were donuts for the staff at the front desk and Mimi would partake. We didn't have donuts often at our house ... but when we did ... she never turned them down.

Erin, the art teacher, told us how Mimi would insert herself into her small art room. I found this so interesting since Mimi hated using her *hands for anything other than eating or moving her wheelchair. Erin thinks Mimi knew the art teacher just needed a hug.*

"I noticed the M&M's in the kitchen," said Christina after dinner.

We were still sitting at the kitchen table. I told her they were Mimi's favorite and how they came to be sitting in the kitchen instead of her room. Christina told us when Mimi stayed for respite at Stoney Glen, she liked to hang out with Mr. Vince in his office. Sometimes he would pull out a small package of M&M's, open the package, and then place a few on the edge of his desk. Then Vince would look away like he was working on his computer. That was Mimi's cue to pilfer his M&M's.

M&M's ... the iconic candy that brought so many of us together.

—

We kept Mimi's ashes at home for four months. Her urn is the shade of baby blue you might see the Blessed Mother wear in religious art and holy cards, and on church statues. My husband made a makeshift shelf across the back of her double bed, which we covered with a blue-and-white checked sheet. We kept fresh flowers on one side of her urn and a small statue of our Blessed Mother on the other side. The small statue used to sit on Mimi's dresser. The wooden blinds were opened during the day and closed at night. Whoever "tucked" Mimi in for the night also turned on her nightlight. I found myself in her room several times a day, just standing, waiting to hear her hum.

It is still so surreal that she is physically gone. Katie and I will sometimes look at each other and simultaneously whisper, "I can't believe she is not here." We both still feel Mimi's presence.

Our son, Ricky, researched Catholic cemeteries for us and found one about an hour away. It was not exactly close by. We met with a representative to see about the possibility of placing Mimi's cremains there about a month after her funeral. But it just didn't feel right. Initially, we were under the impression Mimi must be placed in a Catholic cemetery. The cemetery had severe flooding issues during Hurricane Harvey. There were no niches available aboveground at the time of our visit. There were some niches planned, but no firm date for construction. They did have in-ground spots available that looked like tiny graves. I had never seen such a thing. The granite markers were placed on top of the ground. Because of the Hurricane Harvey flooding, lots of the markers had shifted and were no longer level with the ground. This bothered me. I also didn't like that people could easily walk across the tiny stone markers. The only thing we would consider was an aboveground niche, so our names were placed on a waiting list. We were not in a hurry. Mimi's urn could stay in her room until we found the perfect place.

—

I met with our parish priest a month later for some guidance. He recommended a nearby cemetery only twenty minutes away. It was not a Catholic cemetery. Father TJ explained that when the remains were interred in the ground, or other resting place such as a niche, there was a ceremony performed called the Rite of Committal. It was blessed by a priest or a deacon.

As we sat across from each other, I also mentioned I thought it was interesting that during her funeral Mass he had said Mimi "no longer suffered." I guess I never thought of her as suffering, as she was so joyful. Sure, the early years were riddled with the challenges of physical therapy, orthopedic surgeries, and high anxiety because of her tactile defensiveness. But eventually things calmed down. Even during orthopedic surgeries and recovery, Mimi didn't seem in pain. She never complained. She rarely cried about stuff like that. Mimi, like Christ, knew how to suffer well. Oh, there were emotional triggers, like a few drops of rain falling on her head, or someone else crying, but I never saw these things being associated with pain.

Father TJ mentioned that when he was in seminary, a priest professor had talked about suffering servants. It was his belief that God asks some special souls before they are born to be his suffering servants. I could indeed imagine Mimi having a nice little chat with God. Yes, she would agree to suffer for him to teach other people important life lessons about God's unconditional love and the amazing value of every life.

Mimi told God yes. I feel certain she did not even hesitate with her answer. Mimi taught us and those around her lots of life lessons.

—

I made an appointment with a nice lady at the funeral home adjacent to Rosewood Cemetery in Humble, Texas. She showed me the places on the cemetery grounds that would make the most sense for Mimi. Most were different areas outside. I felt there were definite possibilities for where Mimi could rest and took lots of photographs to share with Rick. It was also peaceful and close by. We would be able to visit Mimi often if this turned out to be her final resting place.

One of the spots the lady showed me included a beautiful mausoleum that looked like a large chapel, but it contained aboveground niches and crypts in the walls. The floors and walls were a beautiful shiny white granite, or maybe marble, and there was lots of glass allowing natural light. There were niches on two walls, with stone fronts containing names and dates carved into the stone. But these same niched walls also contained a number of niches with glass fronts. I liked the idea of visiting Mimi and being able to see her urn. One of the wall's niches had two large glass-fronted crosses, with lots of niches built into them from the floor almost to the ceiling. Unfortunately, many of these niches were already taken. The horizontal niches that formed the cross beam of the cross wouldn't work. Mimi's urn was half an inch too tall. Several niches were high up in the wall. I took a photograph of one niche at the bottom right of one of the crosses. This one was available, but I didn't know if I liked it being so close to the floor.

After I shared all the interment options with Rick that night, he said, "This glass-front niche is perfect. Mimi always had a special devotion to our Blessed Mother. It is as if Mimi will be eternally at the foot of Jesus's cross with Mary."

I don't know why I didn't think of that. It was perfect for Mimi. The more I thought of this spot, the more I liked it for her. I also liked the idea of being able to sit on the floor close to her when I visited.

When I talked to Katie about Mimi's final resting spot, she also chimed in.

"Mom, you know how Mimi never liked to get wet? She will never have to worry about getting rained on," Katie said.

Katie was right. I always told people lovingly that Mimi was like the Wicked Witch of the West from *The Wizard of Oz*. When Mimi encountered rain, it was as if she were melting. It was difficult for most people to believe unless they had witnessed it. Mimi was almost always happy-go-lucky. When I took her out into stormy weather, even with a large umbrella, she would cry or at the very least fuss. Imagine getting Mimi and her wheelchair into a handicapped van in the pouring rain. Both the bus driver and I would hold umbrellas over Mimi, hoping not a drop would touch her. But Mimi, even covered with a rain poncho, would scream bloody murder. The only people getting soaked were me and the bus driver. The crying immediately stopped once she was inside the bus.

I will never forget being at a parade with Mimi on the Fourth of July in our little suburban community. It was so hot, which was probably why a group of kids marched by with squirt guns, wetting down a few people in the crowd. We noticed one of those kids was a friend of Katie's. When this young lady saw Mimi waving at the side of the street, she pointed her squirt gun, and Mimi received a stream of water right in her face. The ensuing screaming was a sight to witness. The young girl felt terrible. She thought the cool water would be welcome.

—

Deacon James had handed Rick his business card at Mimi's funeral Mass and told him he would love to perform Mimi's Rite of Committal. I kept his card for several months, until we had chosen Rosewood Cemetery for her final resting place. Just after four and a half months, Mimi's cremains were interred at Rosewood.

The ceremony was performed in the mausoleum, with lots of family attending. Mimi's sister and brother were in attendance. Mimi's godfather, her uncle Gary (Rick's brother), was there. Mimi's godmother, her aunt Cynthia (Rick's sister), was also there. My brother Pete came with his son, Peter. Mimi's aunt Kathy and uncle Gary came. My sister, Gretchen, of course was there.

Next to Mimi's urn in the niche, there was placed a small photo of a pigtailed Mimi, a holy card of the Blessed Mother, one of her hug cards, and her large chunky rosary beads. Aunt Gretchen placed a small wood-carved cross from Bethlehem. Katie placed a compact mirror for Mimi. Mimi loved to look at herself in the mirror. But not really at herself. If you watched Mimi while she held a mirror, you might notice that she would be holding the mirror and looking behind her. We never knew why she did this.

It was difficult to say goodbye to Mimi. It was only after her urn was placed in the niche that I could look at the face of Jesus on the crucifix during Mass and not cry.

Chapter Nineteen

Life Without Mimi

Don't cry because it's over.
Smile because it happened.

— Dr. Seuss

One of the most memorable notes we received after Mimi left us was written by one of Mimi's school speech therapists, Angie. I think she taught Mimi in middle or high school. The years melt together sometimes. She is also a parishioner at our church. Her words touched Rick and me to the core. It reads as follows:

LESSONS I LEARNED FROM MIMI

- *A willingness to be vulnerable to others*
- *Trusting others to take care of things she cannot do herself*
- *Being present to each moment*
- *Communicating through means other than words*
- *Exhibiting a peaceful spirit*
- *Accepting one's limitations*
- *Showing delight in the simple things*
- *Loving others through a heartfelt embrace*
- *Waiting*
- *A sense of humor*

- *Perfection is in the eye of the beholder*
- *Being a Saint takes many forms — Mimi, in my eyes, is a Saint!*

No doubt, Mimi will be missed. Yet, she waits to greet all of us with that big bear hug!

—

WHAT I DON'T MISS EVERY DAY — I don't miss the lifting. As she entered her teen years, Mimi weighed eighty-five pounds for a long time. That was the last time she was officially weighed. A light eighty-five pounds was an easy lift for me into the back seat of our Suburban. In her twenties, her weight crept up, but we had no way of telling by how much. Some days my back and left shoulder really felt it. My biceps were huge from all the daily lifting.

I don't miss Mimi pulling out her beautiful hair. She had this bad habit of pulling a strand or two from the left or sometimes the right side of her head over and over again. Humming usually accompanied the pulling out of hair. She hummed a lot. Thank goodness Mimi's hair was so thick. It was also the reason I felt a short haircut would have looked oh so bushy and not desirable. I never could break her of the hair-pulling habit. It is why I always had her hair up in a ponytail and clipped back, hoping to discourage the behavior. Often, I would notice a pile of hair strands in her lap and ask her, "Mimi, are you pulling your hair?" Her reply always was "bad," and then she would smile.

I don't miss changing Mimi multiple times a day. She never could tell me she needed to "go potty." The sign language sign for needing to use the bathroom is closing your thumb and fingers into your hand and then shaking your fist. She knew the sign very well, but only used it to get out of doing something. I told myself I would never stop potty training her, though. She had a bedside commode that I used for decades. I would lift her onto it several times a day, put on her favorite television program for a few minutes, and tell her to concentrate. She had great success with a schedule. I often caught her when she was first waking up and still dry! If I was really quick with the transfer from the bed, she would pee a river in the potty. This was followed by lots of high fives as I got her dressed for the day. She was extra proud of herself every time, and so was I. I knew she was more than capable. Her potty was also great for bowel movements. Gravity is a beautiful thing. As anyone who takes care of someone confined to a wheelchair knows, that is the hardest part. All the sitting and not moving makes for chronic constipation, no matter how much juice you drink. In later years, constipation reared its ugly head again. Tweaking her diet helped a lot, but it was always a struggle.

—

WHAT I DO MISS EVERY DAY — I miss going into her room in the morning and seeing Mimi lift her head and say with so much love, "Hi, Mommy." No matter how much was on my to-do list that day, Mimi could put love and family all in perspective with those two little words.

I will miss our funny conversations during her bath time. Taking a bath was not her favorite activity, but we made it fun. It was the whole water thing. The tactile defensiveness got better as she got older, but it never totally left her. Mimi loved for me to sing those preschool songs like *The Wheels on the Bus*, and talk about characters from a television show she watched. She might not have been able to enunciate precisely all the names of the *Looney Tunes* characters, but we both knew what we were talking about. Mimi also adored Vanna White from *Wheel of Fortune*, although I think it had more to do with what Vanna was wearing than how well she turned those letters.

I miss drying Mimi's thick, beautiful hair. She loved to grab me around the waist as she sat in her wheelchair in front of the mirror in our bathroom. She would hold on tight while I moved the brush and hairdryer through her straight, full locks. She loved how, after we were all finished, I put a dab of hand lotion on each of her palms, elbows, and knees. Then a little dab in my own hands, and I would demonstrate how to rub both hands together. She never could quite get the lotion moved around in her palms, so I always helped her.

I miss holding Mimi's hand at Mass. For so many years we sat in the front row so Mimi could see what was going on. I like to think holding her hand had a calming effect on both of us. Mimi could get very excited when she saw a familiar face, and at least I had control over one of her hands. If someone got too close, holding on to one hand usually meant Mimi wasn't going to grab them with both hands, hug them, and then hold on way too long and squeal.

I will miss the high fives Mimi gave me after I picked her up from the day center on bowling day for the past ten-plus years. I always asked her if she beat the boys in bowling. She always said "yeah," and followed it up with an enthusiastic high five. Sometimes I would find out later in the week that their class hadn't gone bowling. Maybe the bus had broken down or the weather was questionable. Time was not something she understood. Mimi lived in the moment.

I will miss her toothy smile. She had a grin that would light up a room. Her two front teeth protruded somewhat over her bottom lip, and her bottom teeth were crowded. She would have been a great candidate for braces if she could have stood wearing them. Her smile was uniquely Mimi and adorable.

I will miss Mimi's humming. I never thought I would say that. After she died, it was the elephant in the room. Our house was so quiet. She had this way of humming that was one very long note. She hummed most of the time unless she had a cold. Or when she was in church. She never hummed in church. Maybe it was the Holy Spirit nudging her to be oh so quiet. Sometimes I wondered if she ever took a breath while humming. And she was really loud. Sometimes I would say, "Mimi, are you humming?" and she might stop … or maybe not. But her little smirk before she started back up was priceless.

And I will miss Mimi saying "I love you," although it really sounded like a sing-song "I wuv you" tune with just three words. But she never could get the rest of the words out. This usually happened spontaneously while I was tucking her in for the night. She learned the lovely phrase from watching way too much Barney. If you have heard Barney, the big purple dinosaur, sing at the end of every episode the "I Love You" song, you know what I mean.

—

There are so many things Mimi has taught me through the example of her life. The love from a perpetual child is unique, so full of unconditional love, so innocent, patient, childlike, pure, especially vulnerable, soft, precious, sweet, spiritual, and lovely. Pure love gushed straight from her heart to mine and to others, so fiercely and freely. Mimi's own kind of special joy left our house when she left us.

Chapter Twenty
Life Is Not for Sissies

Only in the darkness can you see the stars.

– Martin Luther King, Jr.

I met with a grief counselor once after Mimi left us, to work through some things. Six months out, and I was still a mess. I knew this was going to take time. For the first several months, I ran into people in the grocery store, and the crying on both sides started all over again. I learned to keep a few tissues in my purse.

Friends and family have been so lovely to me. I have been taken to lunch, and received loving notes and concerned texts, emails, and messages. People seem to be worried about me. I think they should be. I am worried about me. I can just think about Mimi and the tears spontaneously flow. I think this must feel like that "dark night of the soul" people sometimes talk about. I now know why people say you never get over the loss of a child. Some seem concerned about what I am going to do with all my time now that Mimi is gone. I do not need things to do to fill up my day. My being busy has never been an issue. My life without Mimi has seen a paradigm shift. I miss Mimi's physical presence.

—

And then suddenly, cancer again reared its ugly head at our house a few months after Mimi left us. How could this happen? We had had two great cancer-free years. I soon became fully consumed with dispensing medication, arranging appointments, and planning fun things to distract Rick during doctor appointments and bloodwork, running to MDA's emergency room in the middle of the night, brain surgery, and MRI, CT, and bone scan days.

In February of 2019, we were in the middle of a tsunami. Its name was "brain tumor." Rick's cancer had returned, but this time it had reappeared as a brain tumor. We were hoping getting rid of the tumor would be simple. But it quickly turned into another cancer marathon.

Rick and I had several discussions that perhaps Mimi's death and the brain tumor were somehow connected. Perhaps the physical and emotional stress of her leaving us was too much for Rick's delicate immune system. It was just so strange. He had a clean brain scan before Mimi died. Until a strange and powerful seizure in his left arm appeared on a Sunday in late February, he had been fine.

It wasn't long before things grew more complicated. The gamma knife radiation at the end of February 2019 did not work. The procedure has an 80 percent success rate. We waited for the anti-seizure medications to kick in and the steroids to take away the brain swelling. But they did not.

Next, in June, came a noninvasive brain surgery on the same brain tumor. I hated that the phrase "brain tumor" had become a part of my vocabulary. They told us the success rate for this surgery was also high. In early July, there was another gamma knife radiation for a new small brain tumor. When we finally started stepping down the steroids that were given to combat post-radiation swelling, we were again hopeful. The side effects had not been kind to Rick's body.

At the very end of July, on a Monday, it was discovered during a routine CT scan that Rick had a significant blood clot in one lung and more in the other

We had thought Rick was going to have his first immunotherapy infusion in a couple of weeks to further treat the brain tumor. Instead, he was taken directly to MD Anderson's emergency room and then to the ICU. Katie held vigil with me overnight that first night in the emergency room. Ricky flew in from Michigan, thinking it might be the last time he would see his dad. What would I do without my children and their spouses?

We were living in no man's land. We pondered what would happen next. They told us it was going to take lots of time, maybe six months, for the clots to resolve on their own. The blood thinners' purpose was to not have new blood clots form. Blood thinners and oxygen were started, and then on Friday we went home. We learned blood clots are common risk factors when you have cancer. We added the blood thinner pills to Rick's growing list of medications. Lord, grant me patience.

Then there was the serious lung infection that reared its ugly head in September. Doctors believed the infection could have been the result of a rare side effect from the two immunotherapy infusions that were supposed to take care of the brain tumor. Rick was supposed to have many more infusions. They were put on hold. There were another nine long days in the hospital, piling on medications and tests and high-flow oxygen. Are we going to get through this, Lord?

Another setback occurred in early November when Rick's oxygen dipped way below ninety and refused to recover, no matter how many times he breathed deeply. It was one o'clock in the morning when we left for MDA's emergency room. A few hours into our visit, Rick started having very mild seizures, the first since July. After a chest scan, it was discovered his lungs were again a mess. They were cloudy and looked much like they did in September, only not quite as bad. Had the mysterious lung infection returned? Obviously, he was admitted. There was also a brain scan that revealed the bugger of a brain tumor we had been fighting since February was showing new activity.

During Rick's multiple stays in the hospital, I would go home at night and return in the morning. It was about the fourth or fifth day of the November hospital stay that Rick told me of a vivid dream. Right off the bat this was unusual, as Rick seldom had dreams. Or was it a dream?

"I remember it was very quiet. Then I was in a hallway. It was the hallway to Mimi's room. I looked to the right and saw her large photographs on the wall. There were photographs on the left side. Then I heard someone say, 'Daddy, Daddy.' There were a few more words spoken, but I could not understand what she said. Then I woke back up in the hospital bed," Rick told me.

Rick knew it was Mimi speaking to him. Katie and Ricky had called him "dad" for decades.

After six days, Rick was released from the hospital. He was responding to the antibiotics and was off oxygen again. Before Rick was released, his oncologist, Dr. Campbell, came to talk to us. He was out of tools in his large toolbox for battling Rick's brain tumor. He had thrown everything at the brain tumor and still it came back. We were done.

A representative from a local hospice came to our hospital room. Rick was discharged with antibiotics and anti-seizure medications.

Only God knew the hour of Rick's death. That night we prayed our rosary, adding an intention for a peaceful death and to suffer well. We knew not the day or hour. Secretly, I prayed for lots of good days.

I suggested Rick start writing letters. He started with our grandchildren and then moved on to Ricky and Katie. He wrote early in the morning, before my feet hit the carpet at 6:30. I just stacked them up. I will save the letters to the grandchildren for when they are older. Maybe for their graduation from high school. I was happy Rick had been granted this time to reflect and leave behind words of love, with some "Pop-Pop" wisdom thrown in.

We were grateful for the three grandchildren born during Rick's cancer journey. Our first grandson, Jacob, was such a little guy when Rick was diagnosed with cancer in 2016. Obviously, God knew Jacob needed a little help supporting his Pop-Pop! I have to say, the most memorable birth was Ben, who was born the day Rick was receiving an immunotherapy infusion down the street in the medical center. That was an interesting day!

Our sweet little Zelie, Ricky and Kate's daughter, who is named for a saint, was born on Jacob's birthday in 2018. Then Ricky and Kate's daughter Melanie, named in honor of our Mimi, was born before Christmas in 2019. What a blessing!

I needed to make sure that when Rick left this world, he would be at peace.

—

Nine months after she left us, Mimi would have been thirty-five years old. I don't know how my dear friend Mary remembered it was Mimi's birthday. Some years I can barely remember my own. Mary visited the day before Mimi's thirty-fifth birthday and brought flowers and a lovely loaf of blueberry lemon bread. Mary's daughter, Michelle, and Mimi had been buddies for years. Adorable Michelle has autism and attended the same day center.

Mary and I dreamed Mimi and Michelle would someday live together in a house we would create with two other mothers. We started having the conversation a few years ago, but it never happened. One of the young ladies had a serious health issue, so we stopped talking about it. Our reasoning was always for our girls to live together in their community, with support, before we all died. The icing on the cake would have been that we would have plenty of time to check in on our girls to make sure the transition was smooth.

Although Ricky now lived far away with a family of his own, like Katie, he was always present. He called me the week before Mimi's birthday and indicated he was mailing me something and not to open it until Mimi's birthday. That morning I opened his package, which contained a lovely note and a small statue of the Blessed Mother.

A few days before Mimi's birthday, Deacon James called to chat. The last time I had talked with him was at her funeral, so I was bewildered at the timing of the phone call. I mentioned Mimi's birthday was coming up, and that we would be visiting her at the cemetery. He asked if he could be there to offer a birthday blessing, and of course we said yes. Although he had not been attached to St. Martha in quite a few years, he always had a special place in his heart for Mimi.

Rick and I visited Mimi at Rosewood Cemetery. Deacon James got there before us and had three chairs set up in front of Mimi's niche. He brought his official prayer book with him and offered up a prayer for Mimi's birthday and a prayer for healing, as Rick was still suffering from the effects of the brain tumor.

Afterward, we went to Deacon James's house, which was a short distance away. He lives right around the corner from the cemetery. We learned he made jelly and preserves by the case. He gave us three jars before we left. The only condition was we had to return the empty jars and lids. What a gift we received that day on Mimi's birthday. No wonder Mimi had locked her eyes on Deacon James.

Katie and Chad came to our house with the boys. While we watched the boys, Katie and Chad went to visit Mimi at her resting place. I believe Katie was able to let some of her grief explode while in Mimi's presence. It is difficult when you have little children. She has had to compartmentalize her feelings so as not to negatively impact her little boys.

On Saturday evening, we all went to Mass. St. Martha's office had arranged many months earlier for the Mass to be said for Mimi.

Mimi's thirty-fifth birthday was so sad, yet filled with so many unexpected blessings. I believe divine intervention played heavily into Deacon James calling me a few days before her birthday.

—

I had been avoiding going through the personal things in Mimi's room. I was in no hurry. But there were several things that were easy to part with, like her brand-new wheelchair with the camo on the back. It was an important personal vehicle to get her from here to there. It was donated a few months after Mimi left us. The man who picked up her wheelchair indicated it would be put to good use. I thought he was going to cry when he saw the great condition of the wheelchair. What broke my heart was that it had been so difficult to get her a new one, and she had used it for such a short time.

The double bed she had slept in for so long was also donated. It was where she died and a painful reminder of that terrible, terrible day. I could not look at it without seeing how I had found her that day. The bed and mattress left our house a short time after Mimi's interment.

An entire month of incontinence supplies delivered shortly before Mimi died sat on a shelf in her closet for a few months. The supplies were donated to a nearby nursing home I found, which I thought might have needy residents. When I walked down the long hallway of the nursing home, I knew I had found the right place. The staff were happy to receive the supplies.

We purchased a wooden hope chest to house those important things that were special to Mimi and to who she was. It was delivered a few days after her thirty-fifth birthday. We had it customized to include a brass plate under the lid with her name, the date of her birth, the date she left us, and something special about her. The front of the hope chest has "Mimi" carved into it. A small icon of the Blessed Mother and infant Jesus was embedded next to her name. The icon was given to me by my lovely friend Debbie, who brought it back from Rome. When the time is right, Katie and I will go through Mimi's room and decide what to keep and place in the chest.

—

The church office arranged for a Mass to be said for Mimi on the one-year anniversary of her leaving us. Of course, I was there. It was an early morning, 6:30 a.m., Thursday Mass. It was about the same time of day that I'd found her lifeless little body. I can't believe Mimi is gone. I still expect to hear her humming from her room any moment. The house is a much quieter and sadder place without her.

Rick and I were still praying our nightly rosary a year after Mimi left us. The rosary is a beautiful devotion/meditation to Mary, Jesus' mother, that many Catholics pray with recognizable prayer beads. The rosary is divided into five decades. As we recite the prayers, our fingers move from bead to bead after each prayer is completed. Each decade starts with one Our Father prayer and continues with ten Hail Mary prayers. Each decade has a specific mystery assigned to it.

It was a Friday dedicated to the sorrowful mysteries, representing five events in the life of Jesus, when I started to struggle. The last of the five decades is devoted to the crucifixion of our Lord. Making it more personal yet, the fruit of this mystery is dying to ourselves. While I tried to concentrate on not letting my mind wander that night during the sorrowful mysteries, Mimi popped into my mind. Not only that — tears spontaneously welled up, my nose dripped, and I found myself holding my breath.

Afterward, I had a discussion with Rick about it. I wondered out loud why this mystery was more painful to me than usual a year after she had left us. I wasn't comparing Mimi's passing to Jesus' painful death on the cross, but somehow, I thought, there was a connection. Rick helped me see that we all go through the cross when we die. Christ's crucifixion is a reminder not only of his sacrifice, but also of our own life journey.

Final Reflections

The value of one's life is determined by how much love one gives,
not by how much love one has received.

– Epictetus

Several people have told me it takes a year to begin to get over the loss of a loved one. I feel certain it takes much longer when you lose a child. I mean, children are not supposed to die before their parents, right? I have heard that said many times. And what about a child with so many special needs? Yes, she was very dependent, but she was also so sweet and spiritual. I don't know. The two of us had an amazing spiritual bond.

I can still feel myself holding her fragile little hand at Mass. Until Mimi's ashes were finally interred, I saw her face in the crucifix each Sunday at Mass. Looking up into Christ's face on the cross was something I would avoid so as not to turn into a hot mess at church. Praying the Our Father was sometimes difficult when Rick and I prayed our nightly rosary. I still get choked up when certain songs that Mimi didn't like are played at church. "One Bread, One Body" was a song that made her tear up. When she was beside me, if I was fast enough, I'd pull out my wallet and thumb through some pictures so Mimi could keep her composure. If her lower lip came out, I knew she was like a singing tea kettle, about to blow.

Mimi would also cry during the songs she deemed sad. Maybe it was the slow tempo. We never could figure that one out. We speculated it was the way the notes were arranged in a way that only Mimi would recognize.

She didn't care for the song "Africa" by Toto, where the group sings about the "rain down in Africa." I totally understand that one. Mimi hated getting rained on. But that never explained why "Barbara Ann" by the Beach Boys also made her wail.

I believe we are all born into this world with a mission and gifts. Mimi's mission was crystal clear. She was this little shining light of Christ's unconditional love. I suspect most people got it. People at church like Miss Peggy and Miss Gayle sought Mimi out after Mass and received her hugs on many Sundays. Mimi adored the parade of priests and deacons over her decades at St. Martha. I liked to say she collected them all like charms on a bracelet. Mimi's charm bracelet was very heavy.

Cerebral palsy did not define Mimi. I never thought of her in those terms. She was just our little Mimi. Perfect despite her human imperfections. Neither did her limited intellect define Mimi, as she soared above and beyond in her social and spiritual life skills. It was the world that required Mimi to have lots of labels. Not her mother, father, sister, or brother, or the scores of people who took the time to notice those gifts.

She never learned to read, but Mimi could turn a page and sometimes point accurately to a picture that moved her and be tickled about it. She never learned to recite the alphabet, but if you asked her to call out a letter during *Wheel of Fortune*, it was always a letter, and not a number. Mimi didn't know what numbers were used for, but she could count to eight. Mimi couldn't write her name, but she told everyone whose attention she garnered, "I'm Mimi." Mimi was just one special little soul.

I know many such special souls with special abilities, and they all have a unique story. I could write a book about each one of Mimi's friends from the Village Learning Center. They are all worthy of respect, dignity, and life from conception to natural death. These unique and special individuals have lots to teach us, if only we would pay close attention and tune our hearts to listen.

—

I am again reminded of the story about Pandora's box and the origami version from high school so long ago. Yes, Pandora opened the box and let out all kinds of horrible evils into the world. But do you remember the rest of the story? It seems a small, frail voice cried out from inside the closed box, asking to be let out. Pandora lifted the lid, and the feeble Hope crawled out. That timid little Hope reminds me of Mimi.

Amidst all the evils of the world, it is Hope that offers us joy and peace, endurance, patience, courage, and strength. In life and in death, Mimi continues to challenge us to keep the flame of hope burning brightly.

Mimi in her pumpkin costume at Halloween.

Mimi and mom at San Antonio Zoo.

Mimi at bat during YMCA Special Needs Baseball.

Mimi and mom picking up her new wheelchair.

Mimi and dad before YMCA Bridgefest 5K event.

Mimi and "Ho-Ho."

Mimi and dad enjoy a moment at Galveston beach house.

2014 Galveston beach house family photo.

Epilogue

Sadly, Rick died at home after four months of hospice care, on Wednesday, March 11, 2020. It was also the day the Houston Rodeo was shut down due to COVID-19. The world was about to get crazier.

Several weeks before Rick left us, our great and holy friend Matt and his amazing son, Robert, came to our house for several weeks and helped Rick out of bed and onto the couch. In the evening, they came over and helped him stand up and assisted with getting him into bed. This was no easy task. I do not know how I would have gotten through those rough days without them.

The last week of his life, Rick was paralyzed on his left side and confined to a hospital bed that hospice had supplied. I thought this was our new normal and prepared myself for the long haul. Katie and Chad brought up our grandson Jacob's twin-sized bed for me to sleep on. I needed to be close to Rick during the night. Jacob was only six and happy to help his Pop-Pop with this sacrifice. Jacob slept on a pallet on the floor in his room at home.

There were many blessings on the day of Rick's passing. Katie had been asking me for weeks if I needed a break. Her little family was already providing so much comfort. Without fail, Katie, Chad, and the boys hung out with us on the weekends. But each day was tough. Katie was working full time but offered to come sit with her dad whenever she was needed.

"I'll let you know when things get difficult," I would tell her.

The hospice nurse was dropping little hints Rick might have a few more weeks left, but told me the end was certainly not imminent. It is why I felt secure in scheduling a hair appointment the morning of March 11 and asked Katie to come sit with her dad.

For some reason, the visitors were like spontaneous combustion the day Rick unexpectedly left us. He had so many visitors. Rick's younger brother, Gary, his wife, Christel, and Rick's older sister, Cynthia, all came to visit.

Before Gary said goodbye to his brother, Rick gave him a thumbs-up. That was Rick's last earthly response. Mike Gayle, who had worked with Rick at Shell, stopped by and prayed with us. Our best buddies, Matt, Debbie, and their son, Robert, also visited. I could tell by the look on Matt's face he was worried by the sound of Rick's breathing. I was also. Clare dropped off a lovely meal from the Village.

The most surprising guest was Father TJ. I already had Father TJ on my calendar to visit Rick the following day, on Thursday, March 12. After all our visitors left, Katie and I had a discussion. We had this feeling that maybe Rick was not going to make it through the night.

Starting earlier that afternoon, I had called the hospice nurse several times to talk about Rick's breathing. She had me giving him droppers of medication for pain and anxiety ever more frequently. What started out as every eight hours went to every six hours, then to four, and finally every two hours. Katie and I were making plans to take shifts through the night. But first, we decided to call Father TJ so maybe he could pray with us that Wednesday night instead of coming on the scheduled Thursday.

It has been my experience that when you call for a priest, you never know who is on call. But Father TJ answered the phone. He was at our door in fifteen minutes and prayed with the three of us. Rick was nonresponsive but still breathing. Thirty minutes after Father TJ left, Rick took his final breath. I placed my hand on his chest and felt his heart flutter for a bit.

My brother Pete came to be with us and assisted the hospice nurse with disposing of all the many medications that were lined up like soldiers on a kitchen shelf.

After the hospice night nurse came and went, a couple from St. Martha came to take Rick's earthly body to the funeral home. It was almost midnight. As Rick was put on the gurney, he was covered with a pall, a beautiful quilt made by Martha's quilters, our Prayer Quilt Ministry.

Our Prayer Quilt Ministry had made two quilts for the local funeral home. Our Noreen (we call her "the Fabric Whisperer") designed and organized our merry band of quilters for the special project. The first pall was made in 2016, the year Rick was diagnosed with kidney cancer. I remember assisting with the beautiful, huge quilt with the large, centered cross by sewing on the binding (the finished edge of the quilt). There was a second pall made a few years later. By then I had stepped back from the ministry temporarily due to Rick's health issues. It did surprise me when I saw the label on the back of the quilt. Rick had been covered with the quilt I helped make four years before his original cancer diagnosis.

Rick's funeral Mass was the last event held at St. Martha's Catholic Church before the coronavirus quarantine shutdown was instituted in our area. He is buried close to Mimi. I continue to visit them weekly.

Although Rick lost his painful struggle with cancer, he will be remembered as a great engineer and father who creatively made Mimi's world flat and accessible.

As for me, I am still broken. There are days I believe myself to be on the mend. Writing this book has helped me grieve a great loss. Hopefully, I will someday be remembered for having loved deeply, always learning, and defending mightily.

Acknowledgments

Thanks to my family: my husband, Rick, my daughter Katie, and my son, Ricky, for being selfless and loving, especially when it came to Mimi. We never thought of Mimi as having special needs. She was just a joyful member of our family. Thanks for being real and supportive and, gosh — just amazing human beings. Thanks, Katie and Ricky, for marrying great spouses, Chad and Kate, who continue to humble me with their love and sacrifice during the hard stuff. They melted like the best Tex-Mex cheesy queso into our family from the first day. It is a testament to how they were both raised by great parents whom I also count as close family.

I am so grateful to all of you for reading my first draft about your daughter, sister-in-law, and sister, Mimi. Your insights have been invaluable for the shape and order of this book about a special little girl we all knew and loved so well. I know it could not have been easy to relive some of the hard stuff all over again.

Thanks to my lovely friend and newspaper editor Cynthia Calvert for giving me the opportunity to "write funny" for her so many years ago. She also read an early draft of this book and offered many thoughtful comments.

Thanks to the many extended family and friends, you know who you are, who lifted me so many times out of the pit of despair over the past few years.

Many heartfelt thanks are also extended to David Duhr, at WriteByNight, for assisting with having this book professionally critiqued, edited, proofed, and with the book proposal.

And lastly, thanks to my mom, who taught me how to be a mother.

References

Alfonso, Fernando. "TX Among Worst at Helping People with Developmental Disabilities." *Patch*. January 11, 2019. patch.com/Texas/ dallas-ftworth/tx-among-worst-helping-people-developmental-disabilities.

Frantz, Dixie. "Mrs. Keeling's Class." In *Chicken Soup for the Soul Celebrates Teachers*. Health Communications, 2003.

National Center for Learning Disabilities. "The 30th Mark — A Look at the History of the Americans with Disabilities Act." July 1, 2020. ncld.org/ news/ada-30/.

Scull, Robert. "The Grumpy Bug." A Nick Jr. Just for Me Story. 2001. Narrated by Sandra Bernhard.